Management in the Information Technology Sector 101

What You Won't Find in the University Text Books

**"Management in the Information Technology Sector
101 What You Won't Find in the University Text
Books"**

2010 Lulu, Ronald Stanley. All rights reserved.

ISBN 978-1-4466-5501-6

Contents

Abstract / Introduction

When we go to school, college or university we're taught all about all kinds of things, different subjects such as mathematics, English literature, history, geography, but who teaches you or tells you about what it's like to go to work? What happens and what should you expect? What should I do if I want to climb the corporate ladder? I think many of us go and start work fresh and naive and try to figure it out ourselves as we go along.

This paperback is intended to tell you what the "cynic" sees in the running of companies in the modern working environment and reflects my own observations from 20 years in the workforce, primarily spent in industry and also as a software consultant for several major software firms. I really wanted to address the issues that the glossy ideal images of the corporate world don't want to acknowledge exist, the types of things you'll never find in any textbook on Management in any Library but nevertheless have a major effect on us every day at work, which is a large part of most people's lives. I myself have tired to an extent of reading typically USA produced highly motivationally oriented views of the perfect world and how things ought to be. When I look at the Library shelves there's very little on how things really are in the "typical" organisation. I actually feel that we as humans like to concern ourselves on how things should be in an optimistic sense. We all like happy stories and happy endings, nobody likes unhappy stories and unhappy endings, but in real life good does not always triumph. In the corporate world logic, efficiency, common sense are thought of as "good", inefficiency, lack of common sense and corporate politics are though of as "bad", but we as human eternal optimists by nature like to view the world and we like to hear that good, logic and efficiency prevails, when in real life, this is not always true despite all the glowing reports we read in the newspapers, the financial press and the Annual Reports.

During my working life I have worked in countries such as the USA, Australia, the Republic of South Africa, Papua New Guinea, Hong Kong and Singapore. Although one might expect such diverse countries might provide stark contrast nothing could be further from the truth from my own observations with the exception of Papua New Guinea which I will discuss in the body of the book. It appears to me that work is work, people are people and thinking in companies is thinking in companies where ever you are. These experiences really did provide me the insight that nothing very substantial is different at least in the work place from one country to another.

It is with these thoughts above in the back of my mind that I begin to describe the main issues that confront the reader as they enter and maintain their position within the workforce. While we study at University or College we're taught all about different subject matters, but nobody ever teaches you what it's really like to work in a company which is the place most of us will eventually end up in, one way or another. I attempt to define, give my observations and then give what to me appears to be the explanation that seems most logical under the circumstances for each other the phenomenon described in this book. Of course for many of the issues raised in this paperback there could be other alternate explanations and rationale for the observed behaviour and where I feel this is appropriate I have done so, but where an overriding theme is apparent or the explanation seems to be obvious to me under the prevailing circumstances under which the observations have been made I will stay with what appeared correct at the time. I could have approached this paperback in terms of a thesis type structure, attempting to justify the arguments with facts & figures & statistics to support the arguments presented, but this would have lost the more conversational aspect of the paper that I was looking for. I didn't want this paperback to become so long winded & factual that it became dull & boring to read, but wanted it to be something more like my own personal insights.

I hope that the reader of this paperback will gain another insight into the running of corporation in the modern working environment from another viewpoint that is rarely formally documented, but the thought processes of which are regularly and commonly articulated verbally and culturally by organisations, but never documented because they would be thought to be negative or even embarrassing in most organisations. I think for some of the younger less experienced members of the community, yet to enter the workforce or for those who don't work in office environments these observations will appear unusual and possibly even shocking to an extent as they are at times in direct contrast with the norms of the formal education systems and certainly at odds at times with the dialog that is spruced by the modern organisations and the rosy picture painted by university and college management text books. But I think I can say with certainty that as these people enter the work force and participate over time that déjà vu will bring them back to the pages of this paperback over and over again.

George Orwell in his landmark novel "1984" defines Doublethink to be:

"To know and not to know, to be conscious of complete truthfulness while telling carefully constructed lies, to hold simultaneously two opinions which cancelled out, knowing them to be contradictory and believing in both of them, to use logic against logic, to repudiate morality while laying claim to it, to believe that democracy was impossible and that the Party was the guardian of democracy, to forget whatever it was necessary to forget, then to draw it back into memory again at the moment when it was needed, and then promptly to forget it again: and above all, to apply the same process to the process itself. That was the ultimate subtlety: consciously to induce unconsciousness, and then, once again, to become unconscious of the act of hypnosis you had just performed. Even to understand the word "doublethink" involved the use of doublethink."[1]

It seems strange that Doublethink is apparent in today's day and age, but Doublethink is alive and well in most organisations in that we're lead to believe by our organisations that something is true and we pay lip service and act as if it really and truly is, when we all know inside ourselves that it's not. We say one thing, we project an image consistent with the official verbal message, our actions are consistent also, but deep inside us we know it's all not true at all. Everyone knows this is true, but Doublethink prevents us from anything more than informal complaining about it with our closest colleagues, thinking the whole time that it will never change, it's too hard, the boss won't like it or we're so used to it from other organisations that we've now come to accept that's the way things are and nobody can do anything about it.

I really felt that since many of us spend eight or more hours a day in the office, work is a big part of the lives of many of us today and I felt it was time that the real story be told, that there be a paper you can read that will explain the harsh reality of what happens in the office so you can at least be prepared.

What is Work? Why Do We Work? What is a Job?

What is Work?

Work is hard to define is some ways, some would say that it's the place to go to earn money to live. Maybe the way to finance the recreational part of our lives, maybe punishment to be paid as penance for our recreation, the creation of economic wealth in order to support out modern lifestyles. No matter how you define "work", it means different things to different people and people's motivation to work and why they are there can vary very wildly.

For me, work is something that falls into line for the entire Capitalist systems to work. Profits are driven by the collective input of labour and materials to produce goods which can be sold. Profits allow some individuals to become wealthy and those people become the powerbrokers of society, those who make decisions, those who control wealth creation in some way, but work for most individuals is the input of his or her effort in order to receive a reward in the way of money, money which can then be used to provide the relief of other needs, such as food and shelter in the first instance, but other more sophisticated needs in the more modern society context such as entertainment.

The traditional definitions of work are largely an outcome of the Industrial Revolution in the 19th Century. It conjures images of people working in factories producing physical goods that be picked up and held, put in a box and taken to the warehouse or shop in a truck and then sold. Today the service is the growing type of work and the issue with the service is that it's not storable. The real challenge for companies of this type is to match the customer's requirement with the available services at the same point, alignment means profit, misalignment means failure. Of course the individual can maximize their worth by providing services that are rare and in high demand by customers and employers. The worker providing generic labour in the traditional factory is increasingly under threat from lower cost labour in other countries and also under threat from capital, robotics, factory machinery and such like. There are some in the workforce now whose employment prospects are under threat, but they remain ignorant to this fact and unresponsive to their needs to acquire more relevant job skills.

Why Do We Work?

For many of us work is undertaken because economic necessity, to earn the money to pay the bills and to allow us to maintain a lifestyle. But its not the only reason why people come to work, I know of people that come to work to escape the children at home, which is a personal motivation that not many people would immediately think of and it's not a practice that many of us would deem to be socially desirable but its one of a possible myriad of reasons why people come to work.

Work for some of us fulfils a need to for prestige, especially so with professional workers, some feel that climbing the hierarchy in their organisation will fulfill a prestige need, making them more important people, making them more powerful perhaps, making them feel as though they belong to a higher socio economic class which may in fact be true or some combination of these factors. Some professionals are after a type of self actualization, to be the very best that they can ever be and to achieve the very most that they can ever achieve and work is the mechanism that can allow them to achieve these ends, for these types of people money may not be a strong motivator, but the need to do interesting work may over ride everything else.

Others come to work to mark time because they wouldn't know what else to do with their time if they stayed at home. Somebody like this may appear to colleagues to lack motivation, may appear to be "marking time" in their current position and not appear to have any ambition, but they come to work to socialize to make friends, to provide an interest outside the home, but what motivates this type of person is having a pleasant working environment and pleasant colleagues to work with and it may be that their social circle revolves to a large degree around their work colleagues.

Another group is those that are family oriented, their home lives and their family are the centre of their lives and for them, work is a minor part of their lives. These people may also be hard working, but not really too interested in being ambitious because they are cautious of higher positions that may impinge on their home life and leisure activities.

Yet other older workers might come to work to feel as though they're still contributing to society as a whole. The actually job isn't so important to these people, rather the ability to stay involved in the work force and the ability to feel part of a continuing society are important driving factors.

So there are many reasons why people come to work each day, some of them good for the employer in that they come to work highly motivated, ready and willing to work, but others are not so motivated and present managers in the office environment some challenges.

We Are Defined By Our Work

It has often been said that what type of work we do and how we do it defines us in society and I believe to a large extent this is very true. Society tend to think of jobs as forming a continuum of status with perhaps Doctor or Lawyer at the top end and probably Prostitute at the lower end and people attempt to fit everyone into this span, with the exception of those who have exceptional inherited wealth, Royal families, celebrities and very high ranking politicians and armed forces officers who are regarded as a "breed apart" and not part of the usual society norms.

If you are one of the huge majority of people that lies on the continuum describe then there's a lot we can learn about a person just from their work. This is sometimes called psychographics in the advertising world, but it's true that people of shared background and beliefs will often work together in shared employment groups and this also explains to some degree the popularity of professional organisations. Another factor to contribute to this is that the education systems group us together deliberately into courses and then etch us the same material forcing some degree of standardisation into the collective profession. Another factor to this is that we work with the same people most days at work, they're our colleagues at first but over time they become our friends too and as our friends we spend time together with them, so we can see a collection of many islands of sub cultures developing in large cities that are big enough for this critical mass to be reached in the cities today and it can go some way to explaining why areas are rich and poor in the cities in which we live today.

What is a Job?

A job for many people is a collection of activities that they are asked to do regularly in the work place, but for other people a job may be much more than this, for some the work place, its environment and the people can form the basis for an active social life also, so are in between these extremes. It's not wise to think that everyone views a job as being the same, but it's a mistake made by many people and many organisations resulting in employee dissatisfaction. It's why the term "Culture" has become so important in some companies, they've seen the need for people to view a job in the same way to an extant and in order to keep the staff morale as high as possible, they actively attempt to select and recruit staff who view the job as something more than daily tasks, in fact in the USA in particular it's fashionable to attempt to make the job part of the private life by providing staff with facilities like Child Minding, Gyms and such like, but the practice hasn't really caught on in other countries. In fact, in some countries staff would view this as an invasion of privacy.

A job can also encompass other external things, that really shouldn't be part of the role, but nevertheless are, such as office politics. You need to look at the augmented role, not just the list of items that appear on your job description, because job descriptions can be almost as interesting for what they don't say as for what they do say. It's all about expectation, if you're in a position where there's a few of you carrying the same job description then you'll all be compared, if one is doing something in addition to their job description they'll be thought of as the "good one", the one that wants to strive to help out and provide that extra effort, you have to be conscious of the fact you're being compared to your peers, not just the list of tasks on the piece of paper.

A job is also a changing "living" thing in that that tasks that you'll be required to do will change over time as the needs of the organisation change. It's a mistake to think that the job will always stay the same, especially in today's working environment. Many older workers fall into this trap, because when they were young the work environment was nowhere near as dynamic as it is today and so they're not so used to the concept that jobs can change even if the actually job description may not. Don't expect things to stay the same forever, because they won't.

A job can also be what you bring to the job also in some circumstances. For example, in the highly structured environment, the tasks are very defined and there's little scope for individual influence, but in the less structured environment you actually often have the capability to guide the direction of the job to some extent and if this is the case you should definitely do so in order to show you're the right match for the job. This is often done by those that have some special skill that can directly affect the job and is especially the case for professional workers.

Who Am I At Work?

One of those fundamental things that we should always be concerned with is who we are on the job, are you the right person for the job that you're currently working in? Jobs are constantly changing, the requirements change as the organisation changes and nothing ever stands still for very long. It's vital that you're constantly conscious of the fact that things change, in fact in the past this wasn't true, people stayed at the same job with the same company for prolonged periods of time and working for 20 or even 30 years at the same company wasn't unusually, but in the last 20 years we've seen great changes to this work ethic on both sides of the equation. Employers have become more used to the idea that they can hire and fire when the need arises, but the employee is also more conscious of the fact that they can change jobs for a variety of reasons that suit themselves. Some would say this is a loss of loyalty on both sides but other would argue that this is a "freeing up" of the job market which would be desirable from the point of view of "free market" economics, because in free markets then efficient allocation of resources is assured.

The important thing to remember is that to keep the position you're in, you have to be the right person for that job all the time, even if the job changes, because if that job changes and you're skills don't match anymore then you're a candidate to be eliminated from the role. This may be stating the case is a rather harsh and blunt way, but the reality of the situation is that most companies will give you the rhetoric that their people are the company, that the people are important and that they're all part of the culture that built the firm to the position where it is today, but the truth is, when times are hard and money is scarce the company will have no hesitation to remove you if you're not performing or if they thing you're not required right at that point in time. Your protections lies in your own skill set, you have to attempt to keep your skill set up to date, to keep it relevant and in demand because it's nobody else's business what your skill set is but your own, it's not your employers business and it's not the Government's business, you have to own and actively manage your skills over time because demand skills will change over time, new skills will emerge, old ones will become obsolete. You have to be the right person at the right place at the right time to get the job and keep it.

Actively managing your skill set is sometimes not as easy as it sounds, it's not as easy as taking a course from time to time. The real skill of managing your skill set is to look at the world, outside your company, your job and your existing skill set and ask the questions; "Where is the economy going? Where is industry going? What skills are becoming obsolete? What skills are emerging? What skills are in demand now? And what skills will be in demand in the future?" The answers to these questions can take time to find and can involve some real research as well as some intuition, just observing the trends out there in the world, but once you can answer those questions you can plan your acquisition of skills and ensure you're competitiveness into the future.

Office Hours

The concept of "Office Hours" is interesting more in what is not said about the concept rather than what the company you work for does say about it.

Most companies publish "Office Hours" because there is a legal obligation to do so in some countries or because it's traditional to do so, certainly not because they expect you to work these hours, in fact rigid adherence to these hours would imply in most non-Government organisations a degree of "slackness" and poor motivation to the job. This is not nearly so much the case in the Public Sector, although with privatisation hitting the Public Sector in many countries now this is beginning to change to become more like the private sector. What most employees really mean by the publishing of "Office Hours" is that the start time is the time they would really like you to be arriving at work and occasional lateness is generally OK, but the finish time usually bears no correlation with reality at all. What is really meant in the minds of managers, but never openly stated is that you should stay an hour past the finish time to show you're committed to your work, 1.5 hours if you're a professional worker, two hours if you're keen and more than 2.5 hour if you're really trying to show you're working hard for the firm.

In Asia, I've observed that this trend is even more exaggerated, the starts times are generally later than in the western countries but add one hour to all of those observed finish times that I spoke of in the previous paragraphs. The Asian environment seems to be more demanding of the employee time, although from my experience this extra time that the employee spends at work, may or may not really be of any real use to the employer.

Another factor that I've never read anything about but I feel is starting to have an effect at work with regard to the office hours is the fact that it's much easier now than it was before the advent of the internet and cellular phones to waste time at work. Cell phones give us the ability to hide somewhere in the office away from everyone, maybe in a meeting room and talk on the phone and the really big effect is the internet, which means now we can do our banking, our shopping, chat with other people, do non work related research, read the newspaper even at our desks while at the same time giving the outward appearance that we're really working. You could never do that before the internet. What could you do before that? Sit at your desk and read maybe, but that would be rather obvious and noticed quickly I would imagine. I think this effect is part of the explanation in the trend towards longer hours in the past decade or so for office workers. Employers know this goes on, especially because they're doing it themselves but I've seen very little reaction to it in the work place with the exception of some of the chatting programs being disabled for network security reasons rather than work time management reasons. There's a kind of implicit payback, if we work slightly longer then you won't mind us wasting a little time during the day on non work matters?

In some cases, I've seen employee staying back after work to play on the internet, read books, do almost anything work related or not, just to be seen to be at work until a certain time in order to be perceived as good staff. The one thing that does seem to be an exception to this rule is the "work from home" concept that's becoming popular in some niche areas, but I have also observed that some of the employers that advertise that their staff can work from home, really don't want their staff to do it other than on the very odd occasion. The idea that if you're not physically in the building, able to be seen to be working by your boss, then you're not working is still well and truly alive.

What is a Company?

Types

There are many type of companies and throughout this paperback I will use the term company and firm in a general sense, since I'm really referring to organisations in general and where it's appropriate to point out the differences between different types of organisations I will do so, but to come up with some broad categories that I refer to throughout this book:

Private Companies

Public Companies

Public Sector

Military

Non Profit

I will tend to concentrate on the first three since the overwhelming majority of people in the workforce today are in these first three and will touch only briefly on the later two.

Private companies are those in which there is a small group or sometimes a single person that own and run the enterprise, there's no shareholders on the stock market to appease and there's very little separation typically between the owners and the operators, although in theory there could be. These types of companies tend to have few employees, small structures and tend to concentrate on single markets or product lines. Reporting structures are loose as are job roles, but these kinds of companies can be very interesting in that you would typically experience role diversity and such environments are very good for those of us who don't like to work in very structured environments because if you work in this environment you typically have the ability to bring a lot of yourself into your position and workplace as long as the type of business was not so narrow as to stifle the ability to grow. The down side to these companies is that they may in fact be too small to let the employee grow from a career point of view and they may lack the financial resources to provide the latest office equipment to their staff to use because it simply doesn't add up from a cost benefit viewpoint to do so. Under these circumstances the staff at the firm may find their skills going quickly out of date to the point where it's difficult for them to find employment elsewhere after a few years, resulting in decreased job mobility and decreased salary bargaining power in the medium to longer term.

Public companies are those who are listed on the various stock exchanges around the world and these companies are the primary focus of this book. They're usually large by their nature of being on the stock markets and they usually have the concept of the differentiation of ownership and management achieved through the shareholders and the Directors representing the shareholders and then the actually management of the firm. Because of the separation of powers we can often see strange things going on inside these companies not so much at the level that directly takes their order from the Board since they're trying to implement the broad directions given by the Board, but at lower levels the direction is often lost and what happens in reality is not what was meant to happen. The more levels of management there are the more likely the messages are likely to be lost on the way down to the operation staff who are supposed to implement the requests that flow down from the top. Another problem with the many layers of management is that the news that filters to the top is typically overly optimistic since staff don't want to tell their managers any bad news because the bringer of bad news can sometimes be inadvertently punished for the news that's brought, so there's always the tendency to give good news to the boss and a tendency to hide and bury bad news. Often by the time this filtering has happened a few times what the top management hear news that bears no relation to what's really going on and so it's very often observed that the very top management of these firms are very out of touch with what's really going on. This lack of real information colours their decisions and their thinking about the abilities of their staff and their firms, they often think their firms can achieve very much more than they've actually really capable of in reality.

The Public Sector combines some very unique types of themes into a very distinct culture. It also suffers from most of the problems of many layers of management that the Public Companies suffer from but at the same time there's also usually an extremely rigid HR structure in place that influences the every day transactions that the staff undertake. This HR system is so rigid that it forces promotion by seniority and also results in staff being trained in particular orders, pay rises depending upon your job title irrespective of your value and the work you get through and no chance to change the HR rules. In fact, I know many people that have moved from the Private Sector to the Public Sector expecting an easy life only to find that it's so regimented that they can't stand it for very long and they move back to the Private Sector and I know a few people that have done the reverse. An over riding themes are that you never ever say anything bad about anybody, no matter what happens and no matter how bad they are and no matter how destructive they may be to the working process because the person you say something bad about will almost never be fired and they will be transferred elsewhere if there really is a problem. After that they might be transferred into your department again one day and be your boss and then you have a problem, so that is the rationa

Military and Non Profit organisations actually make up a very small proportion of the work force, but each has their own distinct traits that define them and people that work within these organisations for long periods of time pick them up themselves as to anyone who stays in one of these sectors for very long. The one thing that is outstanding about the military is that they training their people very well how to manage people under conditions of pressure, which of course you would expect the military require, but the private Sector requires this also, but it's often overlooked. I believe it's the single key reason why ex military people can make the transition successfully from the military which is a very old fashioned and conservative environment into the Private Sector which is very fast paced and always changing, their ability to manage people makes up for anything of the other differences that they might have to get used to. Also, the ability to manage people under pressure is something which your average business school does not really dwell on for very long if in fact it's mentioned at all but it's an increasingly common situation in the Private Sector these days, especially so as Globalisation hits us all and forces increasing competitive pressure on the Private Sector.

Organisation

The organisation of the firm has a high degree of correlation with how authoritarian the upper management of the firm is. In general, authoritarian management will enforce rigid lines of reporting and accountability which a more relaxed upper management team will allow looser structures to exist like the matrix structure where people actually have double reporting structures. Another factor which has effect on the structure of the organisation is the structure of the tasks that the organisation does, that is, what type of organisation it is and the environment in which it operates.

For example, a factory environment will have structured processes that never vary to keep the production of the same types of good forthcoming continually, often their staff will be lower skilled and will need precise guidance in what they're required to do. In this environment it's critical that everything has it's place and that place is well defined so that the entire apparatus can operate efficiently as possible for the maximum output of the factory, this type of operation requires a most structured environment and one will generally observe that in this type of environment management structures and attitudes will duplicate the actual processes of the plant. Departments will be aligned along the factory processes, as will the management and the management will be autocratic at least to an extant because they're worked their way up through this type of industry and so all they know is lots of structure.

Another example would be a software development company, the tasks will be fluid to an extent because it depends on where you're at in the software development cycle what it is that you'll require your staff to be doing and what that staff will be required to be doing will surely change over time as projects progress. In this type of environment it's critical that the staff not only be highly skilled to undertake the development work required but they also need o be very flexible in what they can do and also be multi skilled because they will be required to undertake various tasks at various times. Again the organisation will be aligned along the process, but in this case the process is changing over time and so you'll find that the management of these types of organisations will tolerate a much more flexible approach to management again because the managers of these types of firms have worked their way up through the hierarchy in this type of industry and of course flexibility is all they know.

So the background of the managers is often determined by the industry in which they're operated in the past and operating right now, but most organisations have a lot of trouble dealing with and understanding the small support staff that don't form the key core of the business that don't fall neatly into these categories. Factory environments often don't deal well with the support staff in the way of professional engineers and computerized machinery programming people because they fall outside the usual roles for the organisation. This problem can also be exacerbated by the fact that the members of the Finance and HR Departments think of these staff as being part of the factory environment and try to apply the same rules to these staff as the actually factory workers even though their way of working and the tasks that they're required to do are very much more like the software development company example above. Often these staff will become very frustrate over time at the rigid application of HR rules to their position and the companies that fail to recognise that these staff are not really part of the factory environment will often experience high staff turnover and often they won't even realise why.

The same applies in reverse with the software company often having a lot of trouble with the management of the administration and shipping areas, again with the result that these staff find that they find themselves in situations which they're managed in a structured enough way for their liking with the staff turnover problem again being the result.

Purpose

The organisation actually has many purposes when we think about what companies are and what they do. Firstly there is the obvious profit driven one, the purpose that the firm is in business to make money and provide a return for the shareholders, but remember that this is the situation for the Private Company and the Public Company only, for the Public Sector, Military and the Non Profit organisations this is not the case and for the Non profit organisation, it was specifically designed not to create profits but to provide cheap services to consumers or to be as charitable organisations. So while it's true to think of companies in the traditional sense as being in business to make money, this isn't the prime motivating force for all organisations. For example, the prime focus of the Public sector would be to provide the community services at a reasonable price and so we would expected the focus of anyone from the financial parts of these types of organisations to be very cost driven rather than revenue driven since this type of organisation would may not have to concern itself with revenue as such. The same could apply to somebody from a sales background in the Private or Public company; they'd be driven by the desire to expand sales to create more revenue. The person from the military back ground may be more driven by wanting things to work well and efficiently rather than having focus on financial matters at all, all kinds of back grounds exist in society and firms exist for all kinds of reasons. So one of the possible purposes of companies is to create wealth through the production and provision of goods and services.

Other purposes of the firm that may be aren't so obvious to us are that firms provide a social atmosphere in which we interact with other, they provide the opportunity for us to learn social skills that we can use outside the office. If we can't get along wit our work colleagues then we probably can't get along with our neighbours and so firms can have a large effect on the social environment and the social consciousness. Firms also as part of the advertising can engage in helping charities with funds and many firms are very keen to be seen as good corporate citizens by helping the local communities in which they operate. This is especially the case for the foreign owned firms that are keen to avoid being viewed as foreigners coming into smaller countries to take all their profits back home to their home country. The taxation departments of various governments would says that companies exist also to pay taxation to help with the development of the countries in which they operate, although many companies manage to avoid doing this by transfer pricing their goods with countries that have very low rates of taxation. So companies can exist for a variety of reasons and it's very important to realise that their motive for existing has great affect on the culture of the organisation, the prospects there are for career growth and the qualities that the managers will be looking for when they do in fact go looking for those to promote and the decide which staff will have their careers progressed. The really important thing to realise is that you must think about why your organisation exists, what it is hoping to achieve, how will it achieve its aims and then you have to attempt to position yourself as closely as possible to those core reasons for existence. Promotion of those on the outskirts of the critical core is unlikely, but promotion of those close to the core reasons for existence and for those close to the core processes that are used in the firm is far more likely over time.

Performance and the Future

Your career aspirations and the Performance of the firm is closely related to the reasons for its existence. The general rule is that it's far more difficult to progress in firms that are not performing well than it is for those that are doing well and progressing well. When firms are doing well, the goods feeling is pervasive, it becomes part of everything, part of pay rises, part of the rhetoric and part of the ability of staff to move up the ladder, but then the reverse is also true when things are not going well for the firm. Not going well is also pervasive and finds its way into all aspects of the organisation. I've seen on many occasions when things aren't going well the firm will quite rightly go into defensive mode, which means that pay rises are frozen for the staff, natural attrition is allowed to take it's path and as staff leave of their own accord they're not replaced, sometimes there's redundancies and a general feel of glumness and gloominess falls over everything that the organisation is attempting to do. When this occurs then the staff morale will drop very quickly and the result is that staff feel very uneasy, especially when you arrive at work to find some of your friends aren't there anymore because they've been made redundant. Under these circumstances then the natural thing for the staff to think is that perhaps their future isn't very secure here and so that start to look around for other work that might be more stable. People look for jobs and if the firm is not doing well compared with other in the same industry then staff loss will begin to occur, the same applies to professionals, if their profession is doing well, but their firm is not doing so well, they staff loss will begin. This staff loss can become anything from a trickle to a torrent and if the torrent begins then the firm really is in trouble as all their knowledge begins to walk out the door and settle with the competitors. In a way lack of success feeds upon itself and bad predictions of the future can in a way become self fulfilling to the point that the firm can really end up in some enormous financial trouble.

The same can apply to good new, it also can be self fulfilling as staff become excited about the good predictions of the future, but the key thing to remember is that they good news can't be hollow promises. Too many firms try to use this as a way to motivate their staff, giving wonderful predictions of the future and then when it all doesn't visualize the resultant drop in morale can put the firm into a worse situation with their staff than they were in the first place, so wonderful predictions of the future have to have some kind of truthful and factual basis behind them, but when they do things can really go well for firms.

Another way to incent staff based on the performance of the company is the use to Stock options which were in the recent past very widely used in the .COM type of companies. Stock Options can certainly attract the best staff as people are looking for the quick dollar and those with an eye to their financial future can be easily motivated by the use of options, but they can under some circumstances become double edged swords. For example, during the Tech boom of 1998-2000 software companies would give options to their staff in many cases as a partial substitute for salary with the reasoning that the shares would increase and the staff would reap some of the benefits. This would motivate staff to join the firms of those whose shares were increasing and the firms that were in key niche markets that were expanding could use this to attract the very best talent and not necessarily pay any more in the way of salary than any other firm. At the time it appeared to be a classic win/win situation where the company and the staff member received benefit, but it only holds for as long as the share price increases. During 2001 as the stock market dropped, especially the case for IT firms, may staff saw the value of their options drop to zero and then their strike prices were increasingly above the market price. Under these circumstances then the use of Stock Options had almost become an incentive for these staff members to leave because their options were showing no sign of being worth anything in the near future, in these circumstances it could make more sense to leave, go to another employer who could issue stock options again, but this time at a more current market strike price. This situation places the firm in a dilemma, do they let good staff leave or do they reprice the options to a more current market price? To let good staff leave is not good for the future of the company, but then to reprice options is almost admitting to the market that the shares are unlikely to recover their value in the near future, which may give a signal contrary to the message that the management of the firm wanted to give to their stock holders. The best decision isn't easy but as firms attempt to answer this issue the best staff start to leave to find lower priced options elsewhere.

One way to think of this is that it's a kind of natural order that firms that are not doing well should eventually shrivel and die and those doing well, in growth market should flourish and the movement of staff between these firms is also part of that natural order, but then being part of the firms that are shriveling and dying is never easy and the obligation of the management of these firms is to attempt to maximize the wealth of the shareholders, that is to attempt to stop the shriveling and dying from occurring if in fact that is possible in a case by case basis.

Making Decisions

Making decisions can be far more difficult for the firm than you would imagine at times and it can be very difficult for the individual manager at times depending on the circumstances also. No matter what, there's always a myriad of conflicting interests and factors to consider and there's always different management styles, differing objectives to factor into the process and usually the thing that makes it all the more difficult is that decisions are usually required in a time frame that doesn't allow the collection of all the information that the manager would need to make the decision properly. This point is very often overlooked or at the very least underemphasized by the management text books you typically find on the University Bookshelf. Under these circumstances some managers feel it's all too hard to make decisions and actively try to avoid the situation, in fact I had one manager myself who was particularly guilty of this. He was extremely risk adverse and had a lot of trouble handling conflict and would go to enormous lengths to avoid situations of conflict which his staff knew and they would deliberately use this against him. In the end we would joke that he was a manager who had launched thousands on "indecisions", but really it was no laughing matter for the firm, even though the staff found it all very funny. Eventually because this manager would inevitably "sit on the fence" with every single issue that confronted him, he eventually earned the reputation, quite justifiably that he could never decide to do anything, over time the performance of his Department suffered and he was demoted but the company, he correctly interpreted this as meaning that his future career options with the firm in questions were very limited and he choose to leave and pursue other career options. Had he been able to handle his fears of conflict and risk he might have been able to avoid this unfortunate ending to the story.

The previous story really does emphasise the importance of decision making ability for managers because dithering being unable to make decisions will nearly always result in failure and it's true to say that a poor decision implemented well will triumph over a good decision implemented poorly and one of the main things to remember when making decisions in real life is that you'll almost never have all the information at hand that you'd like to have, you'll nearly always have to make decisions with an element of "gut feel" being part of the equation, but it's also important to remember, even if your final decision ultimately turns out to not to have been the 100% best possible option, if you implement well, then the outcome should be beneficial.

The other side of the coin to consider with regard to decision making is the issue of being too autocratic. Many new managers fall into this rap, in fact I would go as far as to say it's one of those classic signs that you see in people who are acting as managers for the very first time, because the thinking tends to be that now you're a manager you're in charge and you have to decide things and tell people what to do. Of course there's an element of truth to this, but at the same time you have to consider your environment and the people that you're working with before you start to do this too much and before you start to do this at such a small level of detail that your staff start to feel like you're impinging on their ability to perform their every day work. Some managers go so far with making decisions that their staff start to feel as though they have no autonomy over the tasks that they're doing and this can especially be the case for professional staff who are more suited to a management style that sets direction for activities rather than setting the actually tasks at a minute level of detail to perform. Being a good decision maker is itself something of an art because part of the art is deciding which decisions to leave to your staff and which to undertake yourself, but remember shying away from all decision making will always result in disaster, not just for the firm but for your own career progression. The key is to use the information that you do have well, knowing you won't have all the information, take calculated risks and be sure no matter what, to implement well.

Culture

The whole concept of Culture in the office is a very much maligned and misused term in my experience. Many firms advertise on the basis of having a unique "Culture" which is advertised to promote and provide all kinds of wondrous opportunities and benefits, but the reality is that virtually none actually deliver on these promises.

I sometimes wonder whether the management of the firms that advertise the wonderful elements of their corporate culture actually believe what they're saying or whether they know there's a hollow ring to their rhetoric? Or whether they're actually so out of touch with what's actually happening at the operational level that they really do believe that it's all true and they're living in blissful ignorance in their ivory towers.

One software company that I worked for made a very big deal about their culture being unique, very employee oriented and that they made an effort to make sure that their working environment was one of the best. They even went as far as touting their awards that they'd receive to this effect which at the time sounded very impressive. After accepting the position I was introduced the HR Manager who gave me the same idealistic talk on my very first day and then I was put to work and after about two weeks I realised that the place was absolutely no different in any way to anywhere else that I'd worked. The whole culture thing at this organisation was completely illusionary, it was all part of the sales spiel that was given to the customers as part of the idea of buying "the company" as a part of buying the software. The story that the employees were given was very consistent with what was fed to the customers, like it was part of an orchestrated campaign from the head office to give this attitude and impression to the customers, but internally none of it was true at all. In fact I would go as far as to say this was in fact the most dishonest firm that I've ever worked for and the idea of the culture being so special was all a kind of unusual con job that was fed to both prospective staff and customers alike. My warning would be to be very careful of the truthfulness, accuracy and sincerity of any firm purporting to have a unique employee oriented culture, I believe that the tern "Culture" is often used these days as a kind of nice and trendy excuse for lower than industry average wages and annual wage increments.

Culture can take many forms and it's very important to your own job satisfaction that you select a job in a firm whose culture matches the type of culture that you're most comfortable with, just as it's important for the firm to select staff that suit the culture that's prevalent. A meeting of both employee and firm on the issue is important to ensure both employee satisfaction and also employee performance.

Another factor which can seriously affect culture is the country of origination from where the management of the firm are from and the country of origin of the firm itself. Sometimes matches that you would think would work may not work, this can be the case with countries that you would even expect to have very similar cultures. If I take the case of the USA, the UK and Australia, these countries share similar backgrounds, common languages, common political and legal systems to a large degree but different management styles are in effect in the office. A very common mistake that companies make is to assume that the UK and Australian management styles are similar and companies that originate from the USA are particularly prone to this error. The USA management decide usually without any foundation that management styles in the UK and Australia must be similar because the UK settled Australia more than 150 years ago, when the truth is that Australian management styles are very much closer to West Coast USA than they are to the UK. The UK manager is typically extremely more formal than Australian staff are used to and extremely more autocratic. What typically happens is that the UK manager comes into play and the Australian staff start to wonder what this new manager is doing and whether he really understands the local conditions, eventually the usually problems of staff loss will be experienced until that manager is removed. I've seen this occur time and time again and it only goes to show that you cannot assume anything with regard to culture no matter how obvious or intuitively appealing our assumptions may appear to be, always research culture before placing people into positions in other countries, no matter how close you think the cultures will be, it's so easy to get it wrong, just like it's always important to research and understand culture before you yourself take a overseas posting, again, it's so easy to get it wrong.

Office Politics

Often you hear people say that a place is full of office politics and there are many places that have been described in this manner in the real world. But thinking about office politics there's always a few things that are in common that are always tell tale signs that there's an office politics situation in a place, these being:

- A Dive between "Us" and "Them" – unequal treatment of staff be it through salary, promotional opportunity, the ability to work over time for pay, take leave, something discriminatory going on
- Poor Morale
- High Staff turnover
- Employee Satisfaction lacking
- Poor Motivation amongst the outside group
- Manager of person of power having "favourites"
- A culture of staff pushing others aside to be noticed (common in the Public Sector)

Or a combination of some of these is more common.

It's often easy enough to see these factors operating in practice e and when this occurs I believe it's the responsibility of the manager in charge to stomp on it immediately because it can have a very disruptive effect on the operation of the group. Sometimes this won't happen because it's the actually high level manager that's encouraging the situation and I'm reminded of one situation where the manager of a country for this firm was so weak willed that many of the staff had never even seen him and he had a favourite subordinate who he felt comfortable dealing with to whom he delegated almost everything. For her, it was the chance of a lifetime to experience growth in her career both in terms of the roles she would be undertaking but also in terms of salary and promotion opportunity. This firm had a policy of employee satisfaction surveys every six months and subordinate staff would rate their manager, giving a score for the expectation in numerous categories and then a score for the met result, with gaps between the to of more than two being treated seriously. The staff member I question had consistent gaps of eight or more which was almost unheard of by the firm, but despite this she was promoted three times in two years and rumours were circulating the firm about all kinds of things including rumours of sexual favours being done. The real issue here was that there was a policy of office politics instituted by the very top manager who should have been deterring the whole thing. Through his very own ineptitude he was encouraging this and causing enormous dissatisfaction amongst the staff who left in large numbers because they felt that their voices were being ignored, which in fact really was true in these circumstances. It's true to say that office politics like this is present in every office, some more than others, but when it's there, you have to try your best to avoid becoming victim to it by either avoidance or simply by voting with your feet and leaving. A manager with no staff is no manager, but many firms find this out far too late, after good staff have been trained and the firm's resources have been wasted on them because they're now working elsewhere.

In the Public Sector the favourite manifestation o office politics is pushing people aside to be noticed yourself. This can manifest itself in ways such as people speaking up in meetings simply to criticize with no solid suggestions as to the solution. It's very easy to criticize but it's much more difficult to come to the table with a constructive way to make things better, but if you can do this, then it's all the more difficult to argue with you. When you're in this situation, don't just be thinking about what is wrong, but you also need to give you solutions to the issues at hand too. Don't be worried about criticism, others may criticize but without solutions to back the criticism there criticism is hollow. In the public Sector there won't be too many people showing large amounts on initiative due the prevalent culture of the place, if you can do that by bringing solutions as well as criticisms then you'll be standing out from the crowd.

Attitude Towards Alcohol

I really don't want to come across to the reader as being obsessed by alcohol, but I though the different attitudes towards alcohol at the work place in different places was well worth mentioning, especially because of the amount of trouble I've seen it cause. In an extreme case I've seen alcohol responsible for a fork lift driver dying under five tones of metal, so of course everyone would urge that people take a responsible attitude towards alcohol in the work place, but how this is implemented in practice varies widely from place to place and organisation to organisation.

Attitudes towards alcohol and the work place vary greatly across the world. For example in the USA their attitude is almost puritan in that alcohol and the work place aren't a good combination and should never be mixed. It's very common to see businessmen having lunch at restaurants and having a coke or orange juice with their lunch, which in Europe such a thing would be incomprehensible. Some countries such as Australia have an attitude between the two extremes of Europe and the USA, where one or two drinks is acceptable, but anymore is considered to have gone too far and leads to the expression of a "three drink lunch" which means you drank too much alcohol at work to be useful to do anything in the afternoon which I think anyone would agree is unprofessional behaviour. However Japan provides the most unusual insight into alcohol use for a western person because in Japan the businessman is expected to go out after work with their colleagues and in particular their boss and drink so much that they're actually quite drunk, it's all part of the bonding process, but it's taken to the extreme so much that it can cause family problems since the man (typically man, since Japan is still very sexist in many ways compared with the west) will be away from family late most week nights in order to be keeping up appearances to this act of culture.

Of course culture clashes happen when companies move from one country to another, such as a company from the USA opening in Europe a clash over the alcohol culture is bound to occur at some point and sometimes it's handled well and other time not so well, but in most cases a common sense rule needs to be applied because foreign companies have to attempt to form a compromise between their own in house rules and the normal rules of the culture in which they're operating. But managers will be "managers" and I have seen instances where there is rigid adherence to corporate head office rules resulting in an out of step attitude with the organisation and the culture in which it is trying to operate. This can result in both customers and staff feeling that the organisation is not in touch with the local conditions and it's the puritan USA attitude of alcohol free dry days that is the main offender here. Many people are so used to the idea that to drink at all, no matter how small amount is unprofessional that they can't allow themselves to become involved in the local culture. The individual is not really to blame, rather the closed mind set that what anybody else is doing isn't right is the issue.

Social Events

Social Events can really be an experience for those that have never attended Work Social Functions Before. There is enormous ranges in the variation between the types of the events and there's enormous variation between the standards of behaviour that various firms deem to be allowable and desirable at these functions. Social events can under the correct circumstances become ways that you can build relationships across work boundaries that you could never breach during regular office hours during regular office activities. For example, in the office it's rare that you can really have a conversation at any type of level with anyone more than two levels higher than you in your organisation but the pretence of a social function can allow this within reason. You could never directly approach managers of other departments directly at work without the pretence of something directly requiring their attention but again the pretence of a social event cuts these invisible boundaries and allows the unthinkable in the office to be permitted at the Social Event. So, while social events give you the chance to meet and attempt to impress people that normally you have only very limited access too, they can also spell disaster if you let the occasional and especially the alcohol become too much for you, which I've seen on a few occasions.

The standard of behaviour that is accepted by various firms can very a lot from one for the next, even within the same industry. You can shift firm to firms that have similar culture and find that what one firms accepted the other will frown upon, so never think that the culture of the firm will necessarily dictate accepted behaviour at Social Events. A software company that I worked for always prided itself on the high standard of the professionals that worked for the firm and it was true that their daily standards of etiquette were quite high, but once each year they had a conference at a holiday type resort at a very nice location which was run from three to five days. At these conferences the theme was strictly work during the day, but after dinner the standard of behaviour went down hill very fast and huge bar bills were normal as was bad behaviour in the nightclub and also afterwards back in the rooms. The firm's official position on this was that everyone was exercising their own free will after hours and that as long as no property was damaged (which it was on one occasion which the firm picked up the tab for) and nobody was hurt then they were happy to live with the work hard, professional day image and apparent contradiction of the night time chaos that went along with it.

I've also been tow Work Social Events that were frightfully stuffy and staid in the execution which was completely consistent with the firm also and everything in between. I've seen fights at Christmas Parties resulting in dismissals and Court action also. So it's possible for Work Social events to go quickly out of control on occasion. My advise on how to handle to Work Social Event is to always act conservatively, a little more conservative than average should be fine, similarly goes with dress standards at the office, a little more conservative than average is fine, the logic being an extremely conservative stance will not win you any friends and actually cause you o be seen and thought o by others as a "stand out" which will subsequentially make it harder for you to gain acceptance of you colleagues and therefore acceptance of career progression. A radically outrageous standard of behaviour or a scruffy standard of dress will almost always cause a credibility gap and you'll be seen to be unfit for promotion, even though this may have absolutely no effect on your work effort or output. Always remember when you're at a Work Social Event, you're on show to all your colleagues and peers, treat it seriously, it may be called a Social Event, but it's really a Work Function.

Incidentally, the person who started the fight referred to earlier, who was dismissed, who subsequentially appealed his dismissal in Court, at which it was confirmed that even though it was after normal working hours, he was representing his firm at the function because he was wearing a name tag which displayed his name and firm that he worked for. He found out that it was a Work Function the hard way confirmed by Court ruling.

Who Works in Your "Average" Company

People?

It's no understatement at all to say that there's all kinds of people working in most companies and I really mean all kinds, especially the larger the company the more scope there is for different types of people to be there. I see this often amongst those less experienced in the workforce that there's an automatic assumption that the graduate treats everyone the same thinking that everyone at work has the same degree of motivation as the graduate themselves does and this can sometimes be a really dangerous assumption. Also, the type of people you'll encounter can vary dramatically from one organisation to another depending upon the type of organisation, the culture, even things like the industry, whether the industry is a growth or declining industry and even the pay guidelines can have an effect on the type of people that you'll find in some organisations.

I've seen some people at work that are highly motivated, they bring a sense of urgency and high quality to everything they do, but that's the person, not necessarily the position or the company and I've also seen this type of person become gradually demotivated because they were hired because of their enthusiasm, but this enthusiasm was not even close to matching the culture of the organisation which was very old fashioned and really not conducive to the growth of this type of individual, eventually they chose to leave that company figuring that this would never change no matter how hard they pushed because there was too many other pushing the other way and they were correct.

Still, others tend to plod along, doing the minimum necessary, feeling that their work is not really the core focus of their lives and so for them, work is just a way to earn money to live. In an extreme example I've seen one staff member who if given work that they didn't like, or thought it was too difficult or was going to take too long and he just didn't feel like doing anything that day, just threw it all in the bin! Although you might think this kind of behaviour would be totally unacceptable, it was tolerated for months before he was finally dismissed.

Other people have fallen into some kind of rut at work, they've been in the same place for too long, they haven't learned anything new for years and are quite happy to go along doing nothing new or nothing too challenging as long as they can. These people receive a very big shock if they were to be made redundant or if their company were to go bankrupt.

Other people are at work to find new skill sets to sell elsewhere at a later date, so they might on the surface appear to be very conscientious and diligent, but it's only with the view that their stay with the organisation will be very short term. This kind of worker can be perceived by everyone as being the answer to a boss' dreams, but in reality I've seen occasions where companies become too dependant upon a few individuals like this and when they leave there can be serious problems for the firm trying to fill the void.

So when considering the people you work with, your colleagues, don't ever assume for a second that they're working for the same reasons that you are because the chances are they're not. It's true to say that it takes all kinds of people to make up this world and it only makes sense that it takes all kinds of people to make up your working environment also.

The Star

The "Star" can sometimes be very helpful to the firm, but then they can also be very damaging to the firm to under some circumstances. What I think of when I think of a "Star" is typically somebody who has been brought into the firm under the pretence that they have some special skill set that nobody else incumbent has and that they've been brought in with some type of mandate to achieve something that the management of the firm could not envisage the incumbent staff doing. Often, if the Star is smart, which they usually are, then they can us this mandate to achieve something to achieve promotion of their own position in the process, being able to show tangible results at the end of the process which the existing staff may not always be able to do because they're locked into the existing Human Resources Structure and the existing method of assigning their objective at to what they're supposed to be doing which will be much more focused on their daily operational roles.

The very nature of the "Star" is that they attract a lot of attention to themselves because they're doing something different and management is supporting what they're doing, rather than management being rather cold and indifferent which is the usually the case for the more mundane routine tasks that will be doe by the firm. They also usually have the power to enlist other staff members to help in their cause if it's deemed important enough and some of the original mandates actually have allowance for this to e included. The "Star" tends to manage this in one of two ways, they enlist staff that are happy to learn from them and are happy to help, in effect deputies that learn from their new mentor, but they can also try to pick the very best staff that they can find o help them along the way too and this is very fraught with danger. Picking the very best staff that they can find can help them achieve their results with minimum fuss, but then it's these very staff who might feel that they've been "passed over" for the position by the advent of the "Star" appearing on the site in the very first place. Many staff will feel that they've been working away in the positions, working hard for the firm and then when the chance for them to grow in the career happens to come along, then the firm has turned their backs on them and brought in an outsider to do the "glamour' work and leave the incumbents with the drudgery of every day work and in the longer tem this can lead to a great deal of staff dissatisfaction and eventually staff losses as people can feel betrayed by their management and not given the opportunities to grow in their careers. Once this feeling begins then the staff affected start to look around and will slowly drop away one by one as greener pastures are found elsewhere.

The appearance of "Stars" at your firm also gives you the chance to move up behind them with very little risk on your own part, but you have to be really sure that the "Star" has you in mind as their successor when the role at hand is finished and they've moved onto together things because "Stars" usually do no stay too long in one place, They're usually brought in to fulfill a single role and then they move on, sometimes leaving a hole behind that you can fill if you've positioned yourself as their obvious successor. So while "Stars" can be very helpful for the achievement of a single important task, they can cause disruption to the existing structure of the firm and can lead to some staff loss amongst your most talented and enterprising staff member and as such, they should be used carefully, but for some individuals the "Star" can lead to promotion to fill the void left as they leave.

Young Girl in Sales

I realise here I'm probably at risk of being called sexist with the following passages in this section of the book, but what follows is simple statement of fact of what I've seen in the work place in my time there. I sincerely do not wish to offend anybody who might read this paperback so please do not interpret anything in this paperback in that manner as this is not the intention.

The "Young Girl in Sales" is thought of as a recent phenomenon, but I really think that in one form or another it's been going on for more than 20 years. It's based on a simple advertising formula that pretty girls can sell things, especially in male dominated firms and industries. This was the case in the past with television advertising which often features young girls selling all kinds of things tat young girls would typically not use. In the late 19080's in the years of excess this idea permeated into the software industry and it became common place to see young girls demonstrating software for all kinds of male dominated industries and I can remember working for a software company that built software for the mining industry. They had a young girl in sales demonstrating the report writer and some of the customer would literally ask her to demonstrate simply to see her and some would book her time for Consulting Assignments simply to see her. Customers that had never spent any money for years would start to open their wallets when this young girl appeared in the Consulting Group. While her skills were really quite good, she was very inexperienced in the industry in which she was operating and when it came time for her to run courses using the report writer there would invariably be complaints about her industry knowledge. But the result of her sales demonstrations really spoke for themselves as she had inordinate success in selling product and some success in selling Consulting time even thought she really didn't understand the industry at all. The real moral of this story is that for her, she was given the opportunity of a lifetime, recently out of University and straight into Consulting, not into the Consulting firms that hire dozens of graduates and then throw then en masse into customer sites, but a firm with many really experienced and seasoned people. For a young lady with a good degree this type of opportunity really be a great career boost and should never be let pass by if the opportunity presents itself.

People Have Different Backgrounds

Also remember that the background that people have also has a major effect on how they behave and what they're thinking.

One of the biggest differences that I see between the background of people is whether their background has been with the Public Sector or not and also whether they've been with the military or not because each of these unique environments have their own very special ways of performing interaction between each other.

In the Public Sector there's a few golden rules and one of the most telling is that you never ever say anything bad about anyone, no matter who they are, no matter how bad they are and no matter what they're doing. The reasoning behind this is that you say something bad about somebody one day they might be your boss and then you have a lot of trouble. In some countries the Public Service is almost untouchable, even if somebody isn't performing they won't ever be fired, they'll be moved elsewhere and in that kind of environment they could easily at a later point in time be moved elsewhere again, back into a position of authority over yourself! And so to have bad blood between yourself and anyone else is a situation that could prove to be fatal at a later point in time. The other thing that the Public Sector is very strong in encouraging is the concept of length of service. The Public Sector is notoriously bad at rewarding good performance and discouraging bad performance and as a result people are promoted on their length of service in a position. I realise that there's a strong push away from this in some countries at this point in time, but old habits die hard and the culture and the mentality is still there and in some places it won't be removed easily. So the presumption is that after a long time somebody knows what they're doing the most and they've "earned" it the most by their length of tenure and as a result they're the one that deserves the promotion. While this may be the case in the Public Sector, it's much less often the case in the Private Sector, but you would be surprised that there are elements of this in place in some Private Sector organisations as it's seen to be "fair" to promote the longest time server in the absence of any other differentiating factor. Once people shift from the Public Sector to the Private Sector which is happening more frequently I've seen some people have great trouble getting used to the different ethics and culture that exists between the two sectors.

The military also has it's own way of doing things and one of it's key nuisances is that they're very strong on leadership as one would expect, which means when people move from the military to the Private Sector it can be seen that the ex military staff make good leaders, in fact great leaders, some of the best boss' I've ever had have been ex military but they make generally poor staff of those expected to be in more structured and subservient positions. Another thing which did surprise me at first was that the concept of length or service that's so strong in the Public Sector is also very strong in the military also.

So as can be seen there are nuisances that can be detected from the background of the people that you'll work with every day. Of course these two generalizations have exceptions but if we examine of overall trend these generalizations hold strong. The important thing to remember that you'll work with all kinds of people, from different countries, different back grounds and their learned experience over their time at work will make them behave in different ways and react different to the same stimuli. Don't ever assume everyone thinks the same as you do.

Human Resources

I realise that the following sections may appears to be adverse to Human Resources (HR) Departments, but the content is based on true real life experience & while this does tend to go against the modern theories or HR Management in modern companies, HR is where I have personally seen the greatest disparity been the theory that is taught in the University & Colleges & the practice that really happens in the real world.

The HR Department

The HR Department is an usually thing in most large companies, in the past people tended to think of HR as recruitment but then in the 1980's and 1990's the role was much expanded to include such functions as them being the overseers of the Annual Performance Review, being responsible for Succession and Career Planning, Training Management and such like and at that time because the role of the HR Department in most companies was much expanded so too was their budgets and their staff numbers and salary packages. The excesses of the 1980's and 1990's have reversed to some extend this decade due to the harsh economic reality and short term decisions being made to cut costs against possible longer term benefits and so the HR Departments in large companies are fighting the reduction of budget and scope. That is, the people working in this field find themselves in a contracting market which says that some will need to reskill and leave this segment to move onto greener pastures. Bearing this in mind it's easy to imagine that the staff in many HR Departments are very defensive and very sensitive when it comes to the subject of the usefulness of the HR Department and it's with this in the back of their minds that the staff of the HR Department conduct their interactions with the other staff of the organisation, conscious of the fact that there's people looking to cut costs and the HR Department is an easy option for cost cutting in the current environment. Some in the HR Department handle this situation by being friendly and forming good personal relationships with their colleagues as a buffer to try to make the cutting of staff more difficult, whilst other attempt to enforce very rigid adherence to HR Rules, especially surrounding the Annual Performance Appraisal of other staff in the firm, thinking that if they can use this to limit the extent of staff pay rises then they must be seen by their management to be doing a good job and a job that can actually be quantitatively measured, because being able to measure the output and the benefits of the HR Department is a thorough, accurate and fair way is always very difficult, it's not the type of operation that lends itself to the collection of hard data and facts. Of course enforcement of rigid adherence to rules can cause discontent amongst others in the firm and because of this I myself have actively pursued a deliberate policy or working for companies which either did not have an HR Department or in which the HR Department was very weak and confined to the very barest essential functions because in my experience the existence of an HR Department and the associated rules and policies has always been used by the firm (perhaps inadvertently at times) as a shield against pay rises would be fought.

What Does the HR Department Do?

In most companies the primary and traditional function of the HR Department was to coordinate the recruitment function and in the old days the name of the Department was typically something like "Personnel". To this end they're often in charge of advertising positions and conducting initial interviews and perhaps the complete recruitment cycle for non-technical positions depending on the firm. The problem often encountered with this is that in their zeal to prove their worth the HR Department can intrude too far into the process, telling managers which staff they can hire or not and they can also attempt to try and influence the selection to technical staff on the basis and using the pretence of cultural fit. I once worked for an Engineering Manager who complained that the HR Department would tell him who he should hire when this manager was a Project Type Manage in charge of staff working on projects and his main aim for selection was to find people with the right skill sets to complete his project. It was a classic conflict of short term needs versus long term needs. The HR Department had the long tern view in their minds when recruiting, but the manager I knew had the short term project view in his mind when recruiting, but the short term view had millions of dollars profit to the firm riding on its side for the successful delivery of the project.

The HR Department is also typically the managers of the Annual Performance Review. Typically they're attempting to devise a system which can compare different skills and professions, combine this with performance and the budget available to determine the pay rises that can be applied to the staff of the firm. This is always difficult and the result is that specialist staff are always left out of the equation because of the HR Department not being in touch with the special niche markets that exist outside the firm for these types of staff. These types of people tend to be assessed on the basis of their job title rather than their skill sets which may be in very high demand outside the firm, with the result that these staff can be terribly dissatisfied with the entire Annual performance review process because they feel and they really do know themselves that the process has failed because it was designed with others in mind, but all are forced to conform. Of course the result of this is that the specialist staff will eventually find other jobs in other organisations that can correctly identify specialist skills and pay accordingly, these usually tend to be smaller firms or those with much less influential HR Departments.

HR Departments are also typically responsible for the administration of Career and Succession Planning information and policy. Whilst I say they're typically responsible for this function I've never even once seen this done well, or even at all. Most companies have trimmed their HR staff to the extent that these functions are not done properly and there's also incentive for the HR Department themselves to cut these functions themselves in difficult times because the results and benefits are much more long term. I have seen some firms attempt to o this by the preparation of Career Development Plans but generally once these have been drawn up there's usually very little use or action as a result.

Training is also another HR Department responsibility, but this generally extends to no much more than the actually organising of the events and tracking people's attendance and maintaining skills inventories of the staff rather than actual participation in them.

What Do the Staff Think of the HR Department?

In my experience most of the actual line managers think of the HR department as something of a thorn in their sides, using their corporate influence to attempt to become involved with the running of individual departments of the firm. I've seen this type of response from all types of manager from Engineering to Account, Production to Warehousing, Procurement and also in IT; the feeling is much the same. The feeling I've experienced from these managers is that the HR Department is out of touch with the running of the daily operations but they still insist on the imposition of Corporate Standards over these group with little regard to the effect that it may have on the daily operation of the firm.

Line managers also resent the rigidness of the Annual Performance Review because the average manager knows that this tool is generally used to prevent giving pay rises to the staff and it's designed to be used by those direct line managers as the tool to blame if an employee asks why they're not being rewarded. Line managers know that this will in some cases lead to staff loss of their very best staff and often they can predict which staff will leave the organisation and sometimes even when that staff member will leave. This is one of the reasons why I prefer to avoid companies with strong HR Departments, because the good employee will always have a much better bargaining position with regard to salary with their own line manager who knows the hard works that been done and can appreciate the effort rather than a distant HR Department which doesn't really have that daily operational contact with the staff members.

Many staff think of the HR Department as being a bit of a waste of time, as being Corporate staff who serve little purpose to those doing the operational tasks of the organisation in a daily sense. This was especially the case in a large manufacturing company that I worked for, the staff were cynical of the motives of the HR Department feeling that many of the initiatives that were pursued by the HR Department were of little use to the firm, but they were the trendy type of activities that had high profile within the firm. Many staff at the site were very cynical.

48

My experience is that the HR department definitely has an image problem with both the management and the staff at the average site. Much of this I think comes back to the fact that the Annual Performance Review is never conducted properly, the rules are considered too rigid and the process usually does not suit specialist staff. Many at both the management and also the staff level consider the process nothing better than a "bad joke".

HR Managers

The one thing that's outstanding about HR Managers in my experience is that they're very well aware of their own mortality in hard times and as a result that use their best weapons to attempt to try to assure their positions within their incumbent firms, their people skills and their ability to enforce rigidness on the Performance Appraisal system in order to minimize pay rises for the staff and therefore prove their worth to the upper management of the firm.

For the manager of the HR Department there's always the dilemma that they're supposed to be representing the staff to management but at the same time it's hard for them to forget who's the one paying them each month. How can anyone be a servant to two masters and be totally loyal to both when sometimes both have conflicting requirements. I think the obvious answer is that it's not possible. The problems come when its bad times for the firm and the HR staff feel themselves that their own positions are under any kind of threat. Under these circumstances then their natural reaction and I dare say the natural reaction for anybody under these circumstances is to attempt to prove their work in hard dollar and cents terms to the management that are deciding which staff to keep and which can be culled. The issue then arises is how does an HR Department prove it's worth in hard dollar terms when the benefits of good HR Management is quite long term through good training programs, career and succession planning and such like, the only thing that can shoe short term dollar and cents worth of the HR Department to upper management of the firm is to reduce pay rises. So when times are tough for the firm, the HR Department begins to typically act as a shield for which the line management of firm can use to resist salary increments and the rigid adherence to the Performance Appraisal system, no matter how ridiculous and irrelevant it's observance may be in some individual cases is the main tool used to implement the minimal salary growth policy. In stead of the Performance Appraisal being a useful tool to measure performance, set direction for the next year and decide the level of rewards and possible promotion recommendations, the entire focus comes to stifling promotion opportunities and resisting staff personal development because these short term objectives can show hard dollar and cents benefits to companies when times are tough for the firm. The really big problem is that many HR Departments extend this mentality beyond the times when things are tough for the firm into the normal actions of the HR Department in order to show the management of the firm in an on going basis that the IIR Departments is a vital part of the organisation in yielding cost savings. This focus for HR Departments is embarrassingly common and you'll never find this in any HR Management text book, but I've personally observed this on many occasions and many of my colleagues have complained to me very openly about this over time. It's actually one of the reasons why I always try to choose companies that are smaller to medium sized to work for because companies of this size will typically not have HR Departments and so the problem doesn't arise. I always think that your own boos, who you work with every day, who knows your value to the company is much more reasonable to work with and will be much more generous when the annual salary increments are made than a faceless HR Manager who doesn't even know who you are most of the time, whose aim is to prove their own worth to the upper management of the firm by reducing the payroll costs of the staff of the firm.

The other characteristic that HR Managers have to help them maintain their positions is their ability to get along with people, they're generally wonderful "schmoozers" and can mix with people from many backgrounds at all levels of the social spectrum. Because of their advanced social skills they're in a good position to attempt to use the personal relationships they can form to hold their positions. I have seen this fall apart on occasion when there are difficult times and the HR Manager has found themselves in the position of having to defend the company against the very staff they're supposed to be representing and once this does happen then the HR Manager may protect their position for the short term, but the staff will never trust that person again and for them, trying to negotiate with militant staff will never be easy for them after this has happened and the same applies even more so if they ever have to negotiate with any kind of union labour. For this reason there are significant number of staff out there in the workforce that regard HR Managers as being "two faced" people who can never really be trusted 100% to represent the staff of the firm to management. In some industries, the HR Manager is in effect a negotiator between the management of the firm and the union labour, but again, in these types of circumstances the personal integrity of the HR Manager in question must be totally unblemished or meeting of the minds between the union officials and the HR Manager is not likely since there will be mistrust.

Accounting and Finance

Profit = Revenue – Costs

The Finance department in most companies views the world according to this formula; it's the key to the way of thinking of everyone involved in this department. The other thing to remember is that the Finance Department has virtually no control over Sales and Marketing in most organisations, they're left with a relatively free reign to do whatever they like, so Finance regard themselves generally unable to control the Revenue portion of the equation, for them it's magic number they have no effect over, they can only take the number passed to them. What they can affect is the Cost portion of the equation and since their focus in life is to maximize the profit of the company then the reduction of costs is where all their efforts will lie.

Cost reduction can take many forms and in most organisations there are a few easy targets for cost reduction, such as the HR Department and Training, these are often the early targets in any cost reduction scenario because the firm can often trim these areas in the short term with very little effect to the short term functionality of the firm, in fact the short term profitability will increase and it appears that Finance is doing a great job. Other areas that usually come net after this is Engineering and IT because these functions have a similar effect as the HR Department and Training. The problems with cuts in this order is that they provide short term benefit for long term cost. The HR Department and Training are cut first because their detrimental effects won't be felt for a long time and it's possible to make up ground at a later date with increased expenditure. The reason that Engineering and IT are generally next to be cut is that their detrimental effects will be felt before those of the HR Department and Training and catch up can be undertaken but it's more difficult due to the specialised skills of the staff involved. Only after these functions have been trimmed will the other areas be cut such as the operational areas since this can have a direct and nearly immediate effect on the operation of the firm.

One problem with this scenario is that there's tendency to perform one series of cuts, then forget that it's ever happened and then at a later point in time perform another series of cuts. Also, another trend is that cuts are made and then when things get better then the initial cuts are never reversed, eventually impacts start to hit the organisation usually first in the IT area because this is the most dynamic of the areas mentioned. The company due to cuts starts to overwork the IT staff, increasing the load of maintenance work rather than new project work. In fact, the IT Department may be cut so much that the ability of the firm to undertake new IT projects may have in fact been disabled. Once the proportion of maintenance work is increased then the IT staff become dissatisfied because IT staff typically have a high desire to learn new skills and maintaining old systems does nothing for your career prospects, the result is staff loss. The same applies to a lesser extent in the Engineering Department, but the effect can be just as severe. Eventually the organisation has just enough staff to support existing processes and anything new in the way of new projects starts to become more and more difficult for the firm to undertake. Finally apposition is reached where new projects have to be undertaken by external parties who often have very short term views of the customer, profit is their driving force and if their driving fore is profit in the longer term then you're lucky because the contractors will have a long term relationship view, but if their view is more short term, short term profit results, then you're likely to have problems with them attempting to extract as much money as possible for the firm in the short term.

Approval

Most firms generally use their "Approval" process as a defensive shield against which the expenditure of money is to be prevented. Although none would say that openly, it's the chief aim of the process, but the official line would be to say that the Approval processes exist to ensure that the financial resources of the firm are correctly allocated.

In small firms the approval process may be as simple as the signature of a manager with the correct delegated authority, but it can be a highly complex process in larger firms. Smaller firms usually have their financial resources available at the discretion of a very small number of people and so where the need arises to spend money, then the process to have this occur is usually straight forward.

Larger firms though, have larger authorization processes usually involving a number of layers of staff with varying degrees of authority over varying amounts of money both as a protection mechanism against abuse and fraud but also to prevent money being spent too easily. This can of course be taken to the extreme where it's so difficult to spend small amounts of money that the authorization process can be a hindrance to progress. The best example I can think of to demonstrate this point was in my very first job after graduation I had to purchase some minor electronic components for prototyping some electronic circuits that were required in the electronics we were contract to design, build and deliver. The total cost of these items was less than $50, but at the firm I worked for there was only two people authorised to sign for petty cash purchases. I tried for two days nearly full time to get access to these people. Just to make it worse when I first alerted my boss about the issue after not being able to initially access either of these two people, my boss wanted to teach the upper management a lesson in common sense so he told me to do nothing but concentrate on getting the signature required for the authorization and nothing else. After tow days the parts were purchased, delaying a multi million dollar project by two days which must have cost hundreds or even thousands of times the initial purchase. It all comes down to the balance for financial control versus the ability of the firm to react quickly in the allocation of its resources. Some of the very large government owned firms have highly complex approval processes that mean that purchasing decisions, even for smaller items can take literally months and while this kid of decision making process might be right for long term decisions requiring much thought, but they're totally inappropriate for firms trying to make their decisions and act upon them as quickly as possible.

The Budget

The budget is one of the most controversial elements in most companies! In fact it can be so bad in some firms as to drive the manager's of the firm to distraction. I've heard many times complaints from managers to the effect of; "I really don't know why I became a Manager, because I just spend almost ever minute of every day trying to get money to be allowed to get things done. If I don't get the money I can't do anything and if I can't do anything I'll eventually be fired, but then I can't do anything either if I'm wasting all my time trying to get money approved". This is such a common dilemma for managers in today's organisations.

So firms adopt a "Zero Base" to the creation of the budget and this involves the managers detailing in exacting detail usually exactly what they expect to do in the forthcoming year and how the expect to spend the money that is allocated to them. The term "Zero Base" implies that there is absolutely no expenditure assumed and everything has to be justified on a cost/benefit basis before the money is to be allocated. While this sound correct and proper in theory the reality is that it creates an administrative nightmare for those involved since every single activity that is undertaken must be cost justified and often this is not so easy to do on activities that cross several departmental boundaries since only the entire process can have the benefits realised easily and the individual manager is not really in a good position to recognise the exact numbers in the detail required. This is an example of the concept of the Heisenberg Uncertainty Principle. Heisenberg was a German scientist trying to measure the speed of sub atomic particles but he realised the only way to do this was to inject energy into the process but in doing so he altered the speed and so the correct speed could not b observed. He concluded that you can't measure anything without affecting its rate of progress and this is most true in companies. The more you measure something, the more effort you spend collecting the information to create result. In some firms the amount of effort that in involved with the "Zero Based" budgeting approach is not worth the final financial savings. This "Zero Based" approach is responsible for the demotivation of many line managers in the organisation who see that their role has become not managers, but people who spend their lives asking for money to be allowed to do their job. Rather than being assessed on their ability to get the job done, they're being assessed on how effective they are at extracting money from the firm, because the extraction of money from the firm during the budgeting process is the key to having the resources to do their job. Managers who are ineffective at extracting the financial resources from the budget process have nothing with which to achieve and will always be destined to failure.

Another approach taken more traditionally was to assume that the expenditure decisions of the past were generally correct and that there needs to be argument for the approval of additional funds. Sometimes this is done on the basis that inflation is taken into account, or wage growth or both, but sometimes neither. This system does have the benefit that not very single item of expenditure has to be justified, saving a huge amount of paperwork for the managers of the firm, but it does have the side effect that it builds in bad practices of the past. A classic example of this is that many Government Departments go on a spending spree in the last month of the financial year, the logic being that if they don't spend all their money then they won't be given the same budget again the next year, they'll be told that they didn't spend all their money, therefore they don't need to be given the same amount in the next year, so this "spending all your money" mentality is actively developed by the approach towards budgeting and many service providers to Government work their businesses on the basis that this will happens every year.

Both systems have distinct advantages and disadvantages, but the real key for the manager to succeed is that they have to have the influence and the ability to be allocated financial resources. If you can't get the financial resources you'll be constrained and will find yourself in the position where you're not able to achieve anything, eventually you'll be seen as a non achiever even though it's not your own fault. Your ability to achieve is directly linked to the access you have to the financial resources of the firm.

Accountants

Accountants have a generally bad reputation when it comes to their part in the running of the organisation and in some ways it's completely justified. They have one thing that's very much in common with the Hr Manager, they're very aware that their positions do not generally contribute to the bottom line of the firm through increased revenues, it's only through the reduction of costs that they can make a positive contribution to the bottom line and it's with this piece of information in mind that the activity of Accountants begins to make sense. Again like the HR manager Accountants are well aware of their own mortality and that when times are hard the firm will be looking to trim staff from the non core operations of the firm and Accounting is one of those areas that most operational executives would like to trim before touching the operational staff.

The Accountant will always attempt to cut costs to prove their worth to the management of the firm, to both protect their positions and also ensure that their worth is realised and appreciated. While this plan of attack may suit the Accountant and their short term career aspirations it might not always suit the company and its longer term goals. This is one of those times where we can see the long term versus short term clash coming into play. The Accountant is thinking about next year's pay increments, promotion in the next year or two or maybe performing well for a year or two, maybe three at the most and then leveraging from this success to gain better employment elsewhere since this is the easiest path to promotion rather than waiting in the firm where you currently are sitting. But all of these reasons for the activities and performance of the Account are all short term, none of these are longer term, the longer term needs of the firm are being poorly considered when Accountants both individually and also as part of a Finance Department act in this manner. The real problem with this short term mentality is that the easiest way to cut costs is to cut the very functions that the firm needs to have in place for the longer term to ensure success and these are also generally the things that are difficult to catch back up on if you let them lapse for some time. The classic Manufacturing example of this would be the plant

Maintenance budget, which many firms will trim year after year after year. This is a favourite item to attack for Accountants because you can cut this item in the short term in many environments and not see any adverse effects for years until after all those who did the cutting in the first place have left the organisation. Slowly but eventually the lack of maintenance starts to manifest itself in the way of increased breakdown of equipment and that means lost production and lost production can mean massive loss of sales in capital intensive industries. At this point the management of the firm has no choice but to commit large amount of money on new equipment, upgrades of existing equipment and increased maintenance effort but at the same time those guilty in the first place for this situation will usually not be working with the firm anymore. They took their pay rises and better positions or leveraged their "success" to get better jobs elsewhere and left their problems for other to figure out years later. What the Accounting staff are guilty of in this example and what they're guilty of in a lot of real life examples is that they're so obsessed in reducing costs that they're actually inadvertently intent on constricting the firm to the point where it may have to eventually close down by taking the short term benefits and ignoring the long term requirements and the management of the firm is actively encouraging the Accounting staff to do this by rewarding the short term efforts that they're undertaking and not incenting longer term views to be followed.

You Need to Spend Money to Make Money

Any small business man will tell you… "You have to spend money to make money", it's the basic premise behind the creation and running of all small business and while it hold true of all business this idea is very often lost in the murky cloudiness of the large organisation. Large organisation reward short term performance, there's no denying this. Your performance appraisal is conducted usually annually, but some companies are six monthly and some are even three monthly and in difficult times there's always pressure for the staff member to have good new to report in each and every appraisal. As a result, people do all kinds of things that are not really in the best long term interests of the firm in order to have some successes to report when it's time to undertake their performance review. So, with the short term in mind we look at how to increase profits, that is, to increase revenue or decrease costs or some combination of the both. The short term very much favours the cutting of costs, it's easy to control and the impact can be felt almost immediately and there's no extra money that has to be justified and approved during the budgeting process. The increasing of revenue is very much more difficult because of the need for new products, marketing, and advertising and then after doing all these things there's always that chance that the revenue won't increase after all, because competitors may make moves of their own to counter our own moves. So given the choice to cut costs or attempt to increase revenues, remembering that we'll be assessed on our performance and rewarded at most annually, then it's obvious that most staff will tend to favour the short term cutting of costs in order to increase the perception of their performance as far as the financial figures and indicators would have you think.

Performance of the firm in the longer term is critically linked to the correct expenditure on the capital of the firm, be it equipment or information over a long and sustained period and the emphasis that most organisations pay to the short term financial objects really is not conducive to the continued existence of firms in general. In fact there is very great pressure on firms these days to post good financial report every single quarter and this is especially the case in the IT industry where firms are severely punished by bulk selling of their stocks when they miss a single quarter's targets. The management of these types of firms find themselves facing something of a vicious circle where they must continually post profits and meet financial expectations of the markets, but at the same time they must try to provide the sound basis for the firm to continues into the future and sometimes the ability to implement both simultaneously is not possible. Under these circumstances there must be a choice between the short term benefits that are possible versus the long term continuation of the firm and the management of the firm will make a lot of people unhappy no matter what course of action they will decide.

IT

Strategy

It is one of those areas of the firm where vast amounts of money can be consumed to enormous benefit of the firm, but vast amounts of money can also be squandered. I've seen many organisation nominate IT as a strategic weapon to be used against the competitors even when the management of the firm have no IT strategy in place, in fact this is common. I think it's still true these days that many higher level manage still don't really understand the age of computerization and they don't really understand what IT can and can't do to achieve organisational benefit. Many of this older breed of manager seem to think if they're spending money in IT then they're pursuing a successful strategy when nothing could be further from the truth. In fact, spending money year after year on the same outdated technology can in fact seal the fate of the firm that it will continue to spiral into oblivion. In fact there was one manager I had to deal with for several years who steadfastly refused to implement any type of commercial computing into his division on the basis that if people were using computers then they must be playing games and not doing their work, he would only implement process based systems where it could be proven without any doubt at all that the head count could be cut directly as a result of the use of the equipment in question.

Setting strategy for the IT department of the firm is normally done very poorly if at all, in fact many organisations that I've worked for have thought of setting strategy in terms of defining a common hardware platform and common software platform, which while being helpful is not really anything other than representing the efforts to provide volume discounts from hardware suppliers.

IT strategy should be thought of as an integrated strategy for what the firm will be using IT for, how functions will be automated and how this automation will affect the ability to generate revenue for the firm but also how it will affect the ability of the firm to reduced costs. This will include such factors to think about such as the type and extent of the use of packages software such as ERP and CRM type software if it's appropriate and also what type and to what extant should in house written software should be used. Another factor which is almost never considered is how and to what extent should the commercial and the operational systems interact as this almost never happens in real life. There's a great divide between the scope and the operation of the commercial systems and the operational systems.

One of the major impediments to the successful implementation of a sound IT strategy are the IT manager's themselves. Typically there's not much glory in running an IT Departments that uses only bought software and does maintenance type work with little or no development work being undertaken. With this in mind most IT managers are more happy the more IT development they undertake and so writing everything that they can possible write from scratch is always their preferred position, despite the fact that there may in fact be quite suitable pre packaged applications that can meet the requirements. Under these circumstances you might find that the requirements will be tilted away from the capabilities of the bought packages in order to justify the cost of the in house written projects.

Another factor that can affect the ability of the firm to implement a sound and sensible IT strategy in the longer term is that wages in the IT industry can be very directly related to specific product knowledge. Good knowledge and experience in the use and implementation of ERP and CRM packages can mean that you're ability to earn salary will command a premium; so many IT managers will select products on the basis of their ability to learn implementation skills that they can then take elsewhere to command higher salaries. This is also the case with many IT staff, who will deliberately seek work with companies that are implementing these types of systems so that they can gin the job skills to do similarly. In any even the firm can find themselves in the position where they've paid a lot of money to buy systems and train people, only to find that their end result is sub optimal because the implementation was not done well because their staff were using the firm as a kind of "training ground" and then the staff have all moved on to earn more money elsewhere. This is surprisingly common to find when you start to look around.

Programmers

There are very many common urban myths about programmers, who they are, what they do and how they act and I think after working in IT for most of my working career most of the myths have some elements of truth about them! Some of the weirdest people I have ever met in my life are and have been programmers and there appears to be no sign of abatement on this issue.

The typical characterture of a programmer is somebody who was kind of computer nerd at school, they spent all their time studying or in the library reading, learning and practicing their skills on the computer. Some body who was really quite lacking in social skills to interact with other except for their very own small group of other who were very like them and some body also lacking in social graces with little literacy ability except forth ability to use the keyboard well. At work their reputation extends to being people with very strange habits both in their work and also with their at home habits. They also have the reputation of being seen to be doing nothing at work for spells of time, but at other times doing all kinds of ridiculous hours at work in order to make deadlines that may be required. They're also seen to have very little business acumen and are more concerned with their own little work than anything much outside their own little sphere of influence. While there is of course elements of truth to this description it is of course highly exaggerated, but there is very common belief in industry and amongst management of most companies that these generalizations are very largely true. It's because of this that managers find themselves sometimes very unable to deal with these kinds of staff, because they feel that they simply can't communicate on the same level as these types of people. Upper management feel much more comfortable addressing the IT manager who they expect in turn to address the programming staff, but this attitude over time extends the impression to the IT staff that the management of the firm are out of touch with what's really going on in their sphere of work and this being out of touch is very true in a lot of companies.

What a lot of managers don't realise about programmers and IT staff generally is that their caliber in the non IT areas has grown tremendously since the time that the characterture was created. This has mainly been so due to the flow of people with other base degrees to the profession because of the job opportunities that have been present the last 20 years and also because of changes to the curriculum that many IT degrees have at many Universities now, with many Universities including Accounting and Economics to their IT degrees to give the IT staff a background in these areas that often come into play in the business world where they'll be working as programmers initially.

Another thing to remember about IT staff and in particular programmers is that they consistently score the highest on surveys showing staff that have a need and desire to learn at work, but they also score the lowest consistently on their need for social interaction in the work place. These people are happy if they undertake interesting work, that lets them learn, expand their skill base, stay up to date and increase their job skills. In this type of environment they thrive, but the harsh reality is that most non IT companies will have mostly maintenance work for their IT staff to undertake, which means for the IT staff, working away day after day on old outdated technology, maybe there is chance to learn and expand skills, but this will not be with the latest technology, so it shouldn't come as any surprise to find that companies that don't spend on the IT Departments and don't in vest in the newer technologies will love staff quickly and experience high turnover of IT staff. For the IT manager this means that he has to constantly walk the tightrope between the cost of new systems and new technology, the need that the business may have of such technology versus the cost of replacing skills that will leave as technology gets older and budgets are tightened. This is always very difficult to do in practice and so there's always scope to get the blend wrong.

The other thing to remember about these people is that because of their very low need of social interaction in the office, exercises such as team building exercises will often be seen by these staff as a waste of time or at the very least they'll be very cynical of the management motive to instigate such schemes and using team building to attempt to create a nice working atmosphere in an attempt to try and get staff turnover to decrease is a strategy doomed to failure before it even starts with these people. Remember, these types of people are quite unique in their own ways and for top management they can be difficult to deal with and their exact roles are usually not well understood by the management of the firm anyway. As a result, actions undertaken by the HR Departments to try and provide incentive for these people to work hard and the type of rewards that are often decided upon by the HR Department for the firm as a whole can often be very inappropriate for these staff and so the staff turnover can be high and most companies typically report high staff turnover in IT and staff turnover is expensive in the way of recruitment costs to find the replacements but also training costs. In the IT industry the recruitment and training costs are so much higher coupled with the risk that new staff may be learning new skills and undertaking training in order to sell those skills elsewhere

Management Outside IT

Management Outside IT tend to view the IT Department and it's Management and Staff with a degree of misunderstanding and mistrust. To many, the IT Department is a little too mysterious and just a little too much of a drain on the budget for them to really be up to doing good for the firm. What the outside sees is that the staff in the IT Department are paid a lot of money compare with those of other professions and the benefits and result from the IT Department are sometimes not quickly seen or able to be recognised which can lead to a degree of jealousy amongst the other departments of the firm. Also, many user areas of the firm see that IT appear to almost randomly select standards with regard to the type and use of software on site and the same applies to which brands of hardware are to be used. There can be major disagreement when the IT Department has the power to set standards for the types of PC's that can be bought but the actual cost of the purchase of the equipment comes out of the individual Department's budgets because then there's always the issue that the Individual Department wanting to buy cheap clone PCs to get the job done, while the IT Department wanting the sites to standardise on one make and model to reduce the overheads of administration and repair.

Managers outside the IT department also have the view that the Manager of the IT Departments are not very good at managing people since their staff turnover in IT is typically much higher than for the firm as a whole in general. The issue here for the IT Manager is the many firms are not really geared towards satisfying the IT professional very well at all. They may not have the correct technology, the salary packages may not be right, the remuneration may not be right and there may be greener fields elsewhere for the individual. For most firms it's hard to keep IT staff for any length of time because they're always thinking of the future, to increase and better their skills to be able to advance their careers and/or their earning power and staying in the same job, using the same technology isn't the way to achieve that end.

Management outside the IT Department can often view the IT Department as being unresponsive to their needs and this can often be true. This can often come back to the whole issue of what the IT Department is really there to do and this is often not communicated very well to the staff of the site or even to the IT staff themselves. Many IT Manager's see their roles as managing the development of software for the site, while other see their roles as supporting the users of the site and some see their roles as being a combination of the two to varying degrees. But most IT Managers prefer to work with the development and maintenance of their own software since their career advancement is much more linked to development than it is with maintenance work or it is with packaged software. This can result in the situation where the users onsite at the firm may have a very different set of priorities than the IT Department may have and over time the IT Department ill be seen by those onsite as being very unresponsive to their needs simply because the IT Department may see that supporting the users of the site as purely secondary priority. Often this can be the fault of the top management of the firm who may have never really considered the role of the IT Department properly due to their own misunderstanding of what is IT and what should they be doing at the firm. Often this issue is never really addressed very well and over time the IT Department does what it thinks it should be doing and the business does what it thinks it should be doing and there's divergence of the two over time. Eventually there's an "Us and Them" scenario develops where the two don't really work well together even though they're all members of the same firm and in theory should all be working together to make the firm successful in the long term. This is a surprisingly common type of scenario and working every day I see projects that fail because they've been led by the IT Department who have embraced new technology with gusto because they see real benefit to their own careers even though the benefits to the business of the firm of the new technology have not been very obvious. When the time comes for the business to start to use the new systems that have been very diligently worked on by IT for the preceding months the business is left to winder why it was all done in the first place. The business often thinks that the IT Department is out of touch with what the business requires to operate and very often this feeling is quite justified.

Management Inside IT

Management inside IT Department varies very greatly in quality. I've seen some of the very best managers that I've ever worked with as IT Managers but then I've also seen managers that weren't really managers at all, rather administrators or old programmers, in fact there's a lot of old programmers running IT Departments in industry today who may know a lot about programming and developing systems but they often don't know very much about running a department full of people, in fact quite the reverse, the stereotypes of programmers that are technocrats that are happy to be left with masses of work to do as long as they don't have to perform too much human interaction are basically correct in a lot of cases.

Management of the IT Department is a lot for firms are typically programmers that have worked with the firm for a very long time and over the years they've worked their way to the top of the heap and that's how they've become the manager, because there's career limitations to being technical in most firms, you have to become a manager to get the rewards that your years of experience deserve. Specialist skills usually aren't recognised well in most firms and especially the case in firms where the IT Department is thought of as a cost centre rather than forming part of the actually sore business of the firm. So in many of these firms the IT manager has gravitated to the top rather than having actually deliberately following this route as a deliberate career path. Many have been forced to change their direction from technical to management I order to gain better salary deals and gain career progression and recognition, but their hearts still lie in the technical work. In the past many more senior technical staff have been forced to make this choice, to give up technical work and become managers to allow their career to progress and get more senior positions or the accept the lower career status that goes with the technical work. In the IT Industry this has been overcome to an extent with the advent of the "Technical Architect" position within firms which is really quit a senior technical position which in effect allows technical staff to delay that decision by five to ten years beyond when it had to betaken in the past, but in many other professions such as Engineering that choice still has to be faced when somebody has about 10 years of experience. The only way to avoid this decision for many is to make the move from working for industry into working for consulting firms.

Management of IT departments are also notorious for not being good at managing people and this comes back a lot to the type of people that go into IT in the first place. Many of these people have very high needs for career advancement, high needs for learning and extremely low needs for personal interaction. These people are good with computers and not so good with people and so many of the criticisms of the lack of people managing ability of the people in the IT industry is justified in many cases. Some of this can be overcome with management training and it's more and more common to find that the IT Manager had an MBA behind them these days but it's still not enough to presume that because a programmer has been programming for 20 years that they're going to be a good manager. A special case of this is that IT Managers are typically extremely poor at handling conflict, they're just not geared towards conflict resolution and some It staff are aware of this and they can use this to the disadvantage of the IT manager who will often give in to demands that are really not reasonable in order to avoid the conflict situation. There are very many IT managers that are guilty of succumbing to this type of subtle pressure from their very own staff.

There's always problems with the importation of people from outside into senior positions within the firm as the current staff that may have been there for some time may feel that there's outsiders being brought in and promoted above their heads and this in itself may lead to the loss of some staff in some cases, but the reality of the situation is that 'it really should be somebody with the correct type of back ground that really has a desire to pursue that path for the career that's given the job of the IT Manager.

Software Standards

IT standards can cause an incredible amount of extra unneeded cost and functional chaos within firms. May firms give their IT departments the task of setting the standards for the IT Department. This is another one of those cases where this sounds quite logical and intuitively appealing, but again there's tendency for the IT Manager to think of their career, the opportunities, the application and use of technology and how it will affect their staff often before the needs and well being of the organisation will be considered.

Standards are then often set by the IT Department with these considerations in mid and the needs of the business can often come second. Also, the setting and enforcement of standards in the IT field can be used by some IT Managers to justify writing in house systems rather than purchasing bought packages that could result in very much fast implementation times and therefore be used by the business in much shorter time. I have many times myself heard IT Managers say "We're an XYZABC Shop" meaning to them that any application has to be developed using this product or tool set. The benefit for the IT Manager is that it's easy for them to maintain code of the same type but the loss for the business will be that anything that's not developed using this tool set will not even be considered for purchase by the firm meaning that the business can miss out on opportunities. Another reason why this is a bad approach in general is that the IT Manager has used his own judgment to arrive at the conclusion of the standards in many cases or in some cases I've seen IT Manager bring in Consulting firms to make the recommendations and if the final recommendations are not in line with what the manager had in mind in the first place, then a subsequent team of consultant might be brought in and so on until the desired result is found. There's a real risk for the firm under these circumstances that the IT Manager may in fact select the wrong technology for the firm and if this it the case then the firm will be committing a large portion of it's IT budget to a technology that isn't going to last and will have to be replaced not too far into the future. This IT industry is very fickle and new technologies can be embraced quickly but if this technology is not taken up in mass then it can be dropped just as quickly leaving firms with large investments that will never pay off because they will need to replace their investments before they've given their returns. This is very important to consider because the IT Manager may in fact be selecting the standards that are in place for the wrong reasons and advancement of their own careers is the most commonly used wrong reason, the advancement potential for the individual is put before the benefit of the organisation as a whole.

The thing to remember for the IT industry is that there are many standards and they're changing all the time and what's in use today maybe redundant tomorrow. The selection of technology to use and to progress the firm with is a very strategic long term and far reaching decision. Individuals very often make these decisions with more than a little self interest in the process and the individual often has the potential to gain a lot from the selection of products that have high market place acceptance and demand. The individual can greatly increase their earning power under these circumstances but they can often also cause the firm to waste a lot of money in the process.

Software Projects

Projects in the IT Industry have to be the most amazing things that anybody who is not an IT person can ever have witnessed. There are all kind of IT project for all kind of purposes, some are projects in which there is development effort on the part of the firm to write their own systems, so are projects to implement packaged software systems, some are done in house by the staff of the firm themselves, some are done by the software vendor and some are done by consultants or third party integrators, but they all have one thing in common. A very high proportion of software projects fail with dire consequences for firms that have undertaken the time and effort and spent all the money. Much of this comes back to who is running the project from the customer's perspective. The real key things to consider here is: If I'm going to run a project that can run for millions of dollars and involve very substantial portions of the resources of the firm, the success of which can be very far reaching for the continued existence of the firm, would I really want my Project Manager to be experienced in doing the kind of work that is required? Of course anybody who read that sentence would answer "Yes", but it's amazing how often the real life answer is "No", very often the person who the firm identifies to be the manager of this undertaking is simply the IT Manager. While this may be an intuitive thing to do since the project would of an IT basis, it neglects the fact that it's the business of the firm that will be affected and also the business users of the firm that will have to live with the results of this project for the remainder of their working lives at the firm. It also assumes that the IT Manager will be business focused with the long term objectives of the firm in his heart and mind when this is sometimes not the case, it also assumes that the IT Manager is experienced in the running of projects, but we've said earlier that many firms have trouble retaining good IT staff because the bulk of their work is maintenance. So there are lots of assumptions behind this decision and it's quite likely not all of them are true in any one place at any one time.

The in house written project that's being run by the IT Manager is probably the most likely project to fail for the pure fact that it will end up typically being technology driven rather than business user driven. The IT Manager is always looking for new technology, typically he's an "old programmer" and typically he's a technocrat, so the interesting part of the project for this type of person is in the selection and application of the IT technology, not in the end use of the product and so as time goes along it's likely that this project will become more focused on the technology rather than the end result, a classic case of the tool being more important that the machine. The IT staff may well be very happy with the result, but unless there is very strong business buy into the process and user involvement along the way then the outcome is likely to be systems that are either not used or barely used because they don't really fulfill what was originally hoped for. Under these circumstances there's users in the IT field today that can build all kinds or work arounds in order to avoid the IT Department and so these islands of automation will continue and flourish with wasted resources being the final outcome for the firm and lost opportunity and hopes the bad taste left in everybody's mouths.

Some firms prefer to avoid this situation with the purchasing of packaged software where this is in fact possible. There are many packaged software packages in the ERP and CRM market niches and many of these have been successfully implemented with substantial benefits to the firm. When implementing this type of software the firm is faced with the decision of whether they should be trying to do this alone, whether they should be using the software vendor themselves to perform the implementation or whether they should be trying to use a system integrator or third party that specialises in implementation to perform the implementation or some blend of these three options. This is often a difficult decision with the costs and benefits having to be weighed up before the best decision can be made.

If the firm attempts to implement themselves then they have to train the staff intensely since these packages are typically complex to implement, so this approach would save a lot of costs, but at the same time there's heightened risk due to lack of knowledge. Typically firms that take this route fail due to lack or knowledge and staff turnover since many of the staff will acquire new skills and then leave to seek more highly paid positions elsewhere and the longer the project is, the more likely this is to happen.

The firm may attempt to contract with the software vendor themselves to use their own team of professionals to implements, but there are issues with this approach also. There's intense pressure from the market for these firms to be seen to be simple and quick to perform the implementation, since there's market perception that these types of software packages are expensive and difficult to successfully implement. As a result there's often an incentive for the software vendor to perform some very minimal implementation on just a few core pieces of the software in order to claim success to the market. What they've done in effect is "pick the low lying fruit", they've undertaken the parts of the job that are easy to do, easy to implement and easy to gain recognition. From this point on wards, it's going to be more difficult. Also, in the haste to get the system up and running there may not have been much in the way of skills transfer to the staff of your firm and so you're left with a system that nobody can really understand and use to its optimum. Mind you, it's also important that you have the staff there for the software vendor to train also, because I have on very numerous occasions seen the reverse apply where the software vendor has been crying out for a customer to train but staff has not been forthcoming. The software vendor themselves have done everything right and have genuinely tried to perform knowledge transfer to the customer but the customer has not delivered the good to assist in the process. So never think that the software vendor is the bad one, seeking to take advantage of the customer, the reverse can be true just as often.

When it comes to the relationship between the customer and the software vendor, it's definitely a case of a love/hate relationship. In many ways the customer will hate the software vendor because occasionally the software vendor will have no choice but to tell the customer bad news, such as, your bug won't be fixed until the next version or the enhancement you requested has not received the support of other users and so it won't be accepted to become part of the standard package, you need to pay to get this done. There's times when the software vendor will have no choice but to pass along bad news to the customer and it takes the mature minded customer to accept both the bad and the good news.

Customers can also stretch the friendship the other way too. If we think about the power base between the software vendor and the customer, it's initially that the customer has all the power, they're the one evaluating and ultimately buying the system and the software vendors are clamouring over each other for the sale. At this position time the customer is in the position to call the shots and they usually will. Tactics that are commonly in use are to play one software vendor off against the other to see who will give the best deal. Also, the customer can use their position of not having signed a contract yet to get work started and get work for free before things are signed. There is of course a point to which the customer can push this before the software vendor will withdraw, but once the software vendor has invested a lot of money into the deal then they'll be reluctant to drop out of the prospective sale. This a very favourite tactic in use in Asian countries where the customer will say that they're not happy that they're buying a product that has no local support, this will almost force the software vendor to open a small local branch of the firm to conduct the support. Once this happens then the customer will deliberately delay the decision and especially the contract signing as long as possible to deliberately cause the software vendor to incur fixed costs of running the subsidiary in order to dive a hard deal on price. The software vendor will be keen to cut their losses and get the contract signed and get the work started. Many software companies have been extremely hurt by this tactic in Asia.

Once the contract is signed then the power base moves squarely into the court of the software vendor. Now they're in the position to dictate term to the customer, to give them bad news about things and many software firms use the post contract signing phase to attempt to revise the customer's expectations downwards. In many cases the team that the software vendor has assigned to the Account changes as the Sales Team leaves and the Implementation Team arrives and the Implementation Teams soon finds they have the job of living up to the high expectations that have been set by the Sales Team during the Sales pro

The final approach to the implementation of packaged software packages is to use either a System Integrator (SI) or one of the major consulting companies that have dedicated teams for the purpose of implementing packages. Again with this approach these firms are under intense pressure to implement quickly from their respective software vendor and it's important to note and sometimes not known so well that most of the software vendors have partnerships with these implementation firms. The big consulting firms bring deals to the software vendors and in return the consulting firms get the lion's share of the associated consulting work and revenue, so never, ever think that the consulting firm that you're engaged to look at a particular problem are impartial, they almost certainly have arrangements with hardware and software vendors. Of course as the customer you can leverage these good relationships, but also be aware that these relationships can also under some circumstances work against you. Another factor with these implementation firms is that the consulting firms will always be looking to extract more revenue from the customer in the form of the implementation of the product while the SI will be looking to try and gain revenue more I the facilities management area. This will often lead to packaged software implementations that are far more highly customised than would normally be recommended by the software vendor. I have seen many of these kinds of implementations that have been very excessively over customised by the big consulting implementor in the rush to collect extra revenue, I've seen this to the extent that the consulting form has in fact written pieces of code that already existed standard in the system simply because it was asked for and nobody bothered to see if there was something standard to do the job because it represented more revenue. There's always a conflict between the customer wanting the job done quickly at minimum costs versus the drive for more revenue from the implementor. Another trick that implementers use to increase their revenue is by the swapping of staff during the project. At the start you'll met Fred, "Meet Fred, he has 15 years experience working here and here and here, he knows this, this and this and he'll be working on your project and the rate for Fred is $XXXX per day" and at the start you'll work with Fred get to know that he's really good and really knows what he's doing. After a while when things are going along smoothly then Fred brings along a "shadow" to work with him, "Meet Bill, he was three ears experience and he's worked on two implementations before, he's shadowing Fred" and the customer is fine with this because Fred has a helper to do the more mundane work and the customer isn't being charged for Bill anyway and everyone is happy. After a time Fred comes a few days a week because of some type of issue that's arisen and after that he stops coming and the customer has Bill working for them. Bill is fine for somebody with three years experience, but he's not to the standard of Fred who has 15 ears experience and at the same time the implementor is still trying to charge Fred's daily rate for Bill which for them means greater profits because the cost of employing Bill is much less than it is for Fred It's a very, very common scenario with many of the large consulting forms and one that's caused many arguments with the customers. Mind you, if you're Bill, you now have a unique opportunity to attempt to rise to the occasion and try fill Fred's shoes, this may be possible at times in which case you'll heave tremendous chance to learn and grow in your role, but some customer will be more focused on the Financial issues and prevent the process from occurring. This process I actually feel can be come a win/win for the everyone if it's done properly, if the implementor is honest about what's going to happen with Fred and Bill at the site and if when Bill takes Fred's place then the rates paid are adjusted accordingly and the customer is comfortable with the whole process it can work well for everybody, but in reality it's too often the grab for money that is the motivating factor.

Some implementers have worse reputations for attempting to extract maximum revenue from the customer than others, one in particular springs to mind which continually does this to the point where the customer has to virtually threaten court action before they'll leave a site, but then this firm has the philosophy that business doesn't really know what they're doing and so that need to be lead, some of the other firms are much less extreme and much more customer focused than others.

To step away from the actually implementors of the project to the process of the project, the single one thing that's done the worst by everyone in this process is testing! This is often the very final part of the project and because of this it's often the part to have it's time and costs cut when things are critical. I've seen so many projects fail because of inadequate testing that it's just ridiculous and I still see absolutely no reversal of this trend as time goes on. It does not make sense to me that a firm would spend so much money on projects and then when the time comes to test that everything has gone to plan and to test to ensure that the customer will see a working product it's all forgotten about as the software developers who worked on the project scatter for work elsewhere because doing testing work isn't very exciting and not really very conducive to their own individual career progress, but it's the final and most important part of the project and that phase that brings about the logical conclusion of the project. While I think there should be more emphasis on testing it's true that there's nothing to be gained personally from it, nobody pays you more to do testing work, it's just not recognised as it should be and that's a fact of life.

As you can see the whole issue of IT Projects can be very complex and there's always a myriad o factors to consider before deciding on an appropriate curse of action. You always need to try and align the financial resources and needs of the firm, versus the ability of the firm to fully participate in the process and also consider the abilities of the software vendor and the implementor and their conflicting motivations before deciding which course of action is best for your firm.

In all these cases there's opportunities for you as an individual, whether you be very first day out from University or whether you be a professional with 20 years experience. The implementation of bough packages gives you the unique opportunity to learn new and very valuable skills. Skills that are immediately transferable to other firms, be they the software vendor themselves, the implementers or other customer of the same product. This is one of the very fastest ways you can escalate your earning power and so if the chance presents itself for you to become involved in the project to implement these types of packages then you should never miss this chance, even doing maintenance work with these type of packages can significantly increase your earning power. In fact this is so much the case that some customer firms will deliberately not train their staff so that they're no as mobile in the job market as they could be had they received the actual software vendor approved and certified training, since many of these software firms will have official training courses and certification examinations in an attempt to maintain the quality of the their partner implementers, which they will often apply to their own staff in order to attempt to add legitimacy to the process.

Enterprise Packaged Software

Knowledge of Enterprise Packaged Software is one of the very fastest ways that an individual can increase their earning potential! There are many types of this software available and they mainly operate in the ERP and CRM software market segments. These packages are very big, very complex and they take a lot of money to purchase and implement but the potential benefits for the firm in the long term can be very large as well. This is why many firms will spend a lot of time and effort and money on these types of software solutions and for the individual, there's enormous benefit to be had knowing and working with these packages as the skills learned are immediately transferable to other firms and these skills are in demand, even at times when industry is slow these skills seem to always be in demand. The trouble for the newcomer to industry is how to break into the learning these skills.

These kinds of systems are fundamentally a database with predefined tables that can be changed or additional tables added with varying degrees of complexity to achieve this. On these database tables there's an application layer which is typically called a "Tools" environment. These are usually something akin to a programming language that has a forms capability and also the ability to connect to the database either directly in the case of the two-tier architecture or via a Middleware in the case of the three-tier architecture. The forms are made to create the front end that the everyday user uses to add and access the data in the database and the programming language is used to apply logic and business rules at the various required locations which would usually be the events on the forms. Whether the system be Web Based or Thick Client based the ultimate intention of what it's to do and how it's to do it is much the same although the trend in the industry is very much towards shifting as much onto the Web as possible. While mostly taking the same approach each of the software vendors in these space ha various pros and cons with their designs and their Tool sets and each makes a compromise between the provision of functionality "out of the box" versus the ease with which the Tool set can create required functionality. For the technically minded knowing these Tool sets can result in a much increased capacity to earn and sometimes only one or two years experience can in cases double the salary of some of the technical staff.

In the ERP environment there are a few big players that typically operate in the Finance, Supply/Logistics, Manufacturing fields and Payroll/HR and some work in the Manufacturing Equipment Maintenance fields also. An easy way to get into this industry is to work with a firm that's actually performing the implementation of this type of software in the functional areas because typically the IT area will be full of volunteers that will literally be clamouring to be part of the project. Far many people in the more functional areas, they'll b more concerned with their current jobs than participating in any new project. For many people working in the functional areas, there's risk in going to work on anew project, especially a major project that could take then away from their usually jobs for more than a year. Many people working in the own industry in their own professions outside the IT arena will shun the chance to work on these projects because they will be wondering; "What will happen to me when the project is over, my old job won't wait a year, it will have been given to somebody else and after the project maybe the firm won't want me anymore". It's this attitude that can present real opportunities for the newcomer to the firm or the industry to the profession because being new you have nothing to lose, you can go onto this project, learn some really good skills that you can then very easily transfer to other firms and other positions and the types of skills that you can learn on these projects can have a massive effect on your earning power.

The same also applies the CRM packages and although there are not so many opportunities at the moment at the time of writing this book, there's longer term opportunity in the CRM then there is in ERP because the ERP industry is quite mature which the CRM is still very much a growing market segment. Again, all the same rules apply to those in mainstream operations who won't want to participate in the implementation project, it leaves real opportunities for those that want to learn and aren't worried about leaving the firm at a later date.

So if the opportunity ever presents itself for you to become involved with any of these types of projects then you should almost always accept without thinking about it., because not only will you learn high demand skills that you can take elsewhere you can also put yourself into the position where some of the major consulting firms may want to hire you to continue to perform this type of work. Doing a project of this type can literally become a stepping stone for you to move into a successful career in Consulting which for may can represent great opportunity both in the form of financial recognition but also great personal growth in their desired field.

The Web

The Internet or the Web has caused a massive difference to the way that business is done and the way that IT is done in the past since it started to really catch on back in 1995 and 1996. The advancement of the Web has been incredible and I remember when I first used the internet back in 1995 using a text based web browsers using grep commands to search, I remember thinking to myself "this is really goods, it's useful, but it's never going to catch on tot eh general populace because it's too hard to drive for the average user" which at the time when I thought it was probably correct, but once the first graphical based web browsers started to ship then everything changed and the Web industry started to experience massive growth that started to feed the Tech stock boom from about 1997 until 2000. During this time you couldn't miss buying Tech stocks, anything that had the term "dot COM" in it couldn't fail and the NASDAQ market boomed and as that market boomed so did the value of the share options of many of the IT staff employed by these types of firms and millionaires were being made all around. Some firms had created literally hundreds of millionaires through the share options and the generation of wealth seemed to have no ending, but of course when things look like that they're usually unsustainable as was the case with the Tech stock boom. Shares had never ending growth built into their share prices as any semblance of sensible share valuation had gone out the window, o of course when the crunch came it came hard and the resulting impact lasted a couple of years.

Once the crunch came then the IT market contracted and the share prices dropped markedly and 90% share price drops were very common, especially in the hot stocks that had experienced the best of the growth during the boom times. When this occurred then many of the firms which had dubious product offerings or dubious financial backing went broke and thousands of IT staff were without jobs and many of those that did get jobs again did so at greatly reduced salaries. So in a way we were responsible for the massive growth in the Tech Stocks but the problems was nobody really knew when the growth was going to slow and so most of the shares were over optimistically valued. Many of these millionaires were smart enough to sell at or near the peak and retain the profits but many also saw their millions disappear as the prices fell, but never the less, the creation and growth of the Web made a lot of instant millionaires who still retain that position today.

Aside from the Financial aspects that the Web has affected there was also the effect that the Web had on channeling. Many firms started to think about how the sold their products and how they should be selling their products. There's a small core group of consumers that buy everything they can using the Web, but the truth for most consumers is that they use a combination of channels for various type of purposes. We generally use a combination of mail, telephone, Web, visit in person and agents to make our purchases but many firms do not handle the situation well when we start to mix and match the types of ways that we contact the same firm. The growth of the internet made many firms really think about consistency across their channels of distribution and how the deal with the issue of customer data and how it's held and used. This started to bring the advent of the CRM package which was designed in an attempt to address this market need, basing itself on the approach that as much routine work as possible should be done via the Web because the Web is bay far the lowest cost way of performing routine transactions in most cases, with the Telephone costing perhaps 10 to 50 times as much per transaction and Face to Face calling being perhaps 1000 times the cost. For this reason experience in the use and implementation of the CRM package is very likely to be job skill that will continue to demand salary premiums in the near to medium term.

The internet also allowed firms to almost totally replace the concept of the information brochure with on line up to date Web content. Printed paper catalogs became a thing of the past to many firms which helped free up valuable resources to deal with more customer oriented issues and certainly reducing the cost of dissemination on information to the customers. It also allows these days that firms can directly link to their suppliers web sites providing up to the minute information about stock levels for example to the users of systems on site and it's this concept that is driving the Business to Business (B2B) data exchanging and partnership concept that's been sweeping the IT Industry for the most recent couple of years since the Internet Protocol on which the Web is based now allows firms of all kinds to have a common method of transporting files to each other which didn't exist until the recent past.

The Web also brought many average people at home a desire and purpose to buy a home computer which ultimately in the long term will mean greater computer literacy for the population as a whole, especially for the younger generation who will be brought up on computer which means for the older workers, the need to retrain and keep up to date with general computer skills is even more of a requirement than it has in the past. If you don't have general computer skills in 10 years time it's very likely you won't have a job. Remember, it's your own ability to get and retain a job based on your own particular skills set that keeps you employed, it's always up to you every day to ensure that you keep your skills relevant and useful in order to keep that job or to progress to the next level up the hierarchy. Replying on somebody else or the government to do it will almost ensure you end up being one of the long term unemployed.

Major Software Contracts

Software Contacts are unusual things in the business world also. In my experience there's a hug amount of time and money being spend negotiating software contracts for projects to implement packaged software and then once the contract is finally concluded and signed, then it's the customer that will begin the process of breaking the concluded contract, almost from the moment at which the contract is signed.

The thing to remember is that these contracts are being signed by lawyers and also very high level managers who are well in control of the finances of the firm. They working with the software vendor to come to a common understanding of what needs to be done, but the problem for most firms is that the software vendor negotiates this type of contract every day but the firm negotiates this type of contact once every five to ten years or so, so there's often a very large familiarity gap between the two parties. The customer will typically be asking for certain Business Processes to be automated by the software since software is typically sold on the basis of reaping a cost benefit which is easier to justify on a Business Process basis to the firm rather than on a functionality basis for the software vendor. The software vendor will be selling software in modules and there will often be disconnects in this process since how the software vendor sells isn't how the customer wants to buy, but this is often the case. The software vendor will be making commitments about time and delivery of certain functionality at certain times, they know their products and they know the hardware and platforms and have a generally good idea what's needed to set up the hardware and they know the software perfectly since it's their own product. The software vendor is often able to put the customer into a very vulnerable position contractually by insisting that the customer have hardware in place by certain dates and also that the customer provide certain data in certain formats by certain dates. Usually the high level managers will not understand all the background work that will go into making the hardware and data requirement commitments. The high level managers will think of these details as formalities and go ahead and sign, but it's these items that will prove difficult for the firm to meet and ultimately will cause the firm to default on contractual performance. The setting up of hard can be extremely difficult for the firm to undertake because they don't do it often and also in most major organisations the security requirements of the firm require extensive security work be done before a machine can be connected to the firms network. The firm will often default on the delivery of data in set formats because they won't typically have data to suit the structures of the new system that they've bought and to get the data into those formats that have been agreed upon can require large amounts of work. This problem can be made worse for those firms that have outsourced their IT departments because to perform this work required the outlay of "real" money and not an internal cross charge as would be the case for a large firm with their own internal IT Department.

Consequentially, the customer will almost inevitably default on their items that they we're supposed to perform under the contractual agreement and this will then give the software vendor plenty of room to move and argue for tradeoffs. The software vendor knew this was going to happen even before the contract was singed since it's virtually impossible to comply with these terms, but this is a case of when the "devil is in the detail" and the high level managers in their zeal to get on with the job are often duped by the software vendor who has seen this all happen many times before, sometime this is the case but then sometimes it's the customer that's pushing the software vendor as hard as they can to deliver in the shortest possible times and it's the customer themselves that are driving the timeline, even though the timeline is totally unrealistic and the software vendor may know this very well, but high level managers constantly over estimate the abilities of their staff to deliver even when cost cutting of the firm has seen to it in the past that the firm has no staffing ability to handle any new projects at all, they're staffed just to do the every day work that is required to keep the company running along. There's always the tendency of the higher managers to have confidence in their staff that they've selected over time, but also high level manager usually operate in a blissful state of ignorance because their information is typically very filtered from below. The good news from below reaches the top, but the bad news is filtered out, so it's not surprising to realise that the managers at the higher levels have unrealistic expectations of the staff as to what they can deliver and by when.

The Shared Service Centre

What is a Shared Service Centre?

The Shared Service Centre is a very much maligned and misused term to describe a portion of the business that provides services to other core parts of the firm. The term has lost some of it's gloss in the past few years as very many firms have attempted to implement the concept and most have dramatically failed and because such implementations are very high profile when they have failed they've had the spot lights of the corporation right on them when the failure has occurred.

The whole concept of the Shares Service Centre is that it's a part of the firm that runs s if it's a separate business, outside the core operations of the firm providing shared functions that the operational areas of the firm will require, but these functions are definitely not sore to the running of the operation, such as Finance/Account and Payroll being the most common examples, these function are required by all firms but it's the level of service that's not always consistent and this is where those old fashioned Accounting/Finance and Payroll Departments were different and it was this difference in the quality that in the past lead to so many internal dispute as the cost of various services and the actually service levels that are required. There's always the issue that one group will need and therefore demands very high and fast levels of service for some particular task, but to another group this service will be of minor importance and waiting prolonged periods will have no effect on their operations. Traditionally the service group has had to raise to the highest level required and treat everybody the same and while the group that doesn't not view the process as a priority is getting really good service it's not making any difference to their bottom line and for them, they're being charged for a very high level of service that they don't really need or want. The whole concept of the Shared Service Centre is that they can provide the same service to different groups at different prices depending upon the agreed levels of service, so in the example above, the high demand group that really needs fat response will pay a higher price and get a better level of service than the group for which the process is ancillary, they'll pay a lower rate and receive a slower response time. The theory being that once working with the Shared Service Centre is in this manner then you should be able to directly go to the market and compare the prices and service levels that the Shared Service Centre is offering against what is available out in the market place, since in many operations there's complaints that services to the core operation of the business are so high the all the profits are eaten up by the cost of the services provided by the corporate groups in companies. In this way the operations groups can make direct and fair comparison and use this comparison as a bargaining point against the Shared Service Centre if required as some firms will allow outsourcing of services provided by the Shared Service Centre under some circumstances. It should be noted that because the Shared Service Centre is tied whether it be tightly o loosely to the structure of the firm there should be advantages to them over a total outsourcing based on local knowledge, so it were to be the case that outsourcing be cheaper than a Shared Service Centre performing the same work, the outsourcing deal will in reality be cheaper because they would have to place more resource into the process because of the lack of local knowledge.

Problems can be experienced by the firm when outside companies decide to take a "loss leader" approach to the Shared Service Centre, using other lines of business to offer services to the firm below costs to get the work and have the Shared Service Centre lose staff to the point where they can never take the work back on again at a later point in time. Once this has happened then the outsourcing firm is in a position to raise prices and recover their profits and with no effective Shared Service Centre in place in opposition anymore then there can be substantial long term costs to the firm.

The Shared Service Centre does however give unique opportunities for those working in the Services areas of the firm. There are few people in the job market with real experience in working in this type of environment and most of the implementations of this concept have failed because they fall back onto providing the same level of service to all their customers, which means that high service level users will not be serviced correctly and penalties maybe be applied to the firm in accordance with the term of their contract and other customers will be over serviced without any additional payment being received. Experience in a successful implementation of the Shared Service Centre would have you well placed to join a Consulting firm because of the lack of staff with this type of experience and skill.

Service Level Agreements (SLA's)

The real core of the operation of the Shared Service Centre is the use of the "Service Level Agreement" (SLA). This is the real crux of the operation and it's very important the Shared Service Centre have a grasp of its costing structure before attempting to negotiate the SLA with a prospective customer, it's here where this often goes wrong. Too many manager charge into the negotiations of the SLA without really knowing what it's going to cost to provide the service at the level requested by the customer and there's fore they can't really know if they're negotiating to make a profit or a loss. Cost modeling is really important here, knowing each process that you'll be offering and knowing the cost of that service at various levels of service with various response times is critical, otherwise you may be negotiating yourself into a loss even before you've processed the very first transaction.

The other thing to remember is that once you have multiple customers with the same type of service process but with different levels of service in their agreements you're going to spend time to manage that. It's very intuitive to think that you'll gain economies of scale by taking on more customers with the same types of processes for you to support and if they all have the same service agreement then it's the easiest possible case and under those circumstances you're not really a Shared Service Centre, but a service Department, but once there's different levels of service involved and penalties for later service then the management of this can often cancel out the effects of the economies of scale. So it's very important to attempt to get as many customers onto the same service level agreement as you can noting that this will never always be possible, but if you get customer demanding premium services than you have to be sure you're charging to cover the premium you'll be paying on your costs. It's very important where some customers have penalties in their contracts to know the cost/benefit of defaulting on service. It maybe that the penalty that you'll pay is 100 times the benefit you'll receive from correct processing on time of another customers process, but if it means that by defaulting once for one customer you can process 200 of the other, then it may well be worth making the deliberate choice to default on service. This is of course the short term view, there are other longer term factors to consider such as too many defaults will cause the customer to look elsewhere for their service

The main reasons why the Shared Service Centre will fail is the cost of the services is not properly understood and also the cost incurred for the interaction of differing service levels is not understood either, not is the cost/benefit of defaulting on the service of any one customer leading to the situation where the negotiate prices are so low that the Shared Service Level can never make a profit. The management and modeling of these various costing scenarios is a major problem for most Shared Service Centers and it takes a lot of time and effort and cost to establish these factors correctly. To make it even more difficult, these factors often change over time and are affected by such issues as the degree of computerization to the processes being undertake, the experience level of the staff and the familiarity they have with the processes. Also the measurement of the achievement of the SLA is also an overhead that has to be taken into account but many Shared Service Centres don't allow enough resource for this to occur. After all the hidden costs are considered many firms are in the situation where they are wondering if the Shared Service Centre will ever be worth implementing. In general it has to be a really major firm with very large operating Departments that can ever get this to work effectively, for the smaller firms there's too many fixed costs associated.

Self Service

Self Service is another topical issue in Industry because it's through Self Service that costs can be cut and in theory the level of service can be simultaneously increased to the customer by providing information on the internet. At the present there's many companies making great advancement in this area by providing the customer the ability to do the routine things themselves and using their own staff to handle the exceptions that are complex and require human intervention to rectify or action.

For the customer the Self Service concept mean empowerment of their own to a degree, they don't have to reply on others to help them, they're able to access valuable information at any time at any place which is the real crux of the customer getting their better level of service. I know myself that a firm that had a good and helpful Web Site is almost a pleasure but then again, a bad Web Site that's difficult to use or has nonsensical business rules being enforced (which is actually rather common, in fact very much more common than you would imagine) can do the exact reverse and push me to the point where I don't want to deal with that firm anymore. So I feel the use of this type of technology can result in extreme customer experiences, both good and bad as the case may be.

The firm should embrace self-service as much as possible since the cost of doing business over the internet is very much less than the cost of doing business by any other channel so encouraging the customers to everything possible over the internet should be encouraged, but the key to doing business over the internet is that it should be easy for the customer to do this, otherwise they'll fall back to their old channels of dealing with the firm, by telephone or by personal contact which cost very much more than the internet channel. The main issue for firms attempting to do this is that there's always a tendency to cut costs in the development of the web site and the more cost cutting that you do, the more chance there is of things not being done properly and if things aren't done properly when making the web site then there's potential for things to go wrong to the disturbance of the customer. The best examples I can think of is that many sites assume if you're using the same email address as somebody previously registered with them, then you must be the same person and they won't let you register again. This to me, means turning customers away because email addresses expire, especially on some of the more popular free emails sites, the other example that springs to mind was an Australian airline had on their web site if, if you booked a ticket on the web for a flight and paid by credit card, you had to type in all your details which was fine, but at the end there was a radio button for the USA and Canada for the country and if you're from any other country you had to type in the country, even if you were from Australia and that was the airlines home country! This was a constant source of frustration and annoyance for everyone that I knew who used the site, in fact it was plain stupid to deliberately annoy your own customer, in fact the customers that are giving the new technology a try and helping you reduce your costs in the longer term.

So self service is something that I think we'll see gradually increasing over time, it's definitely on the upward trend, so anything you can do to gather experience in this type of work will help your career performance over time, especially in the IT area. In fact this area is growing so much the IT field at this time that the industry as allocated an acronym for this type of work, B2C (Business to Customer).

Does it All Work Together?

At present I'd really like to say that it's all working nicely together, but the harsh reality is that the results have been very mixed and scattered across different industries and across different firms within these industries. One firm in particular stands out in that it's a bookshop with no real physical presence at all; all of its business is done via the web eliminating the need for expensive stores to deal with the public and no sales force as such. This site is seen as one of the leaders in the web sales industry, but having said all that and despite their extremely good web site which is often used by other firms as a kind of bench mark against which to measure their financial performance of the firm has not really been that good, all things considered, so it's sad that the very best example that I can think of has not really succeeded financially.

It's also nice to know that the airline that was mentioned in the above example has also redesigned its web site and fixed that very obvious and annoying problem, so maybe it was the response of the customers that prompted the reaction.

Some other examples have had mixed reaction and I have personally seen a few of these projects fail because the web site was designed with very many cost constraints cutting the final results to the point where the customers wouldn't use the final web site. This is really pity since there was a lot of cost put into these projects and the final results were very disappointing for everybody concerned.

At this point in time it may be better to concentrate on the intranet for many firms with large staff numbers because for these firms the intranet provides a good entry to use and design of web sites for mass usage. It's much better to learn and gain experience working with one's own employees rather than use the customer base to experiment with, so the intranet can be a valuable testing ground for companies as well as providing real cost benefits in the way of staff being able to find information for themselves reducing the information dissemination that normally has to be done by the service parts of the typical organisation. The same applies to partner firms and their staff, it's much better to gain experience with those who know us and will be forgiving of some small mistakes than risk upsetting customers. It's all a question of risk versus return, the intranet has lower return in almost all cases but the risk is also s very much lower.

I'm sure as organisations develop some maturing in the use of this concept and as the software vendors also mature in the availability of the software tools to produce these kinds of sites the success rate of the whole Self Service concept will increase and even now we're seeing some very good sites produced that have had major impacts on the running costs of their business, but it's also true to say that as yet there's not too many good examples to speak of, I'm sure this will be an very much expanding arena in the next decade.

The Boss

Friend or Foe

Your boss can be many things to you in the work place, they can be your friend, your foe, your mentor, they can be somebody who helps you progress but they can also be somebody that prevents you from progressing. Some of this you can affect and some of it you can't, some of it is simply imposed on you by the boss, the firm and the culture of the firm and sometimes there's absolutely nothing you can do about it, because that's the way that the firm operates.

In most firms that I've worked for the boss has been a quite reasonable person, somebody whose job it is to get the best performance possible for the firm using the resources that they have available to them and that's the key to how most boss' think. The resources they have available is what they have for them to get ahead, so if you can be thought of as a valuable resource then you almost won't be able to anything wrong in your boss' eyes, but if you're not thought of that way then it's time to fin another job because staying won't be pleasant. It's always very nice if you can find out quickly what is that your boss is being rewarded for and what's they incented for and if you can find this information out when you're more than half way to having your boss as your friend and ally. If you can find out what is exactly that your boss is being measures on by their management, then you can position yourself to be as helpful ass possible towards achieving this ends and also, if you can find out what incents your boss you can position yourself accordingly there also. It's very important to remember that incents you to work may not always incent your boss and bosses aren't always incented by more money, especially if they're middle level manager in non sales parts of the firm. It could well be that your boss really values being able to take occasional time off, so if you're responsible enough to be able to run things for a day or two occasionally, then you're more worthwhile in your boss' eyes than somebody more productive, but not able to manage the responsibility of running the operation, even in a quite passive way in their absence.

Most managers have reached their positions in the private sector by being able to make decisions and so, in the private sector managers will decide quickly and quite decisively which staff they think are good and which they don't think are good and once this decision has mentally been made by them manager it won't be easy to change this line of though. Remember, in an earlier section of this paperback I said that a bad decision implemented well will yield a better outcome than a good decision implemented properly, well this is the case for the thought process of the manager when it comes to the mental evaluation of staff. So it's very important that you get off to the right start with your boss or manager, the wrong start can take a long time to recover from if at all. Some managers also feel that they're compelled to act on their evaluations immediately and so will do things like implement performance improvement plans for staff that they don't feel are up to the mark in order to provide some type of excuse at a later point in time to having that staff member removed from the organisation, but the truth of the matter is that if your manager ever talks about improvement plans, it's time to find another job, because they've already decided you're not to stay whether this decision be justified or not. I have actually seen this happen first hand to a colleague who had that bad start with their manager and the improvement plan was implemented by this manager who values his own decision making ability so much that he always acted in this manner. The staff member attempted to transfer to another part of the firm but found that he was prevented from doing so and so was eventually let go. He did however launch court action against the firm for a "wrongful dismissal" on the basis that he was not given opportunity to prove himself adequately and this was in fact common knowledge amongst many within the firm. Eventually an out of court settlement was made. After this experience, the manager in question "restructured" his group so that there was an intermediate level of management between him and his direct subordinates and this action of in effect removing himself from the front line action of the firm and placing himself more distant from the staff resulted in much better harmony for that group. In this case the manager himself could see his own inability to manage staff and so shifted the rules so that other would take that role for him.

If you have manager to get onto the good side of your boss, then working for the firm can be an absolute pleasure, not to imply that in any way this gives you an excuse for not working to achieve superior results for the firm, but the actions of your boss will tend to be supportive, something to help you strive to reach your best, rather than destructive when you're trying to collect evidence to ensure your protected from your boss. In the destructive case, the staff will waste time attempting to create cover for themselves because they know that they can't rely on the help and assurance of the manager and this was particularly the case for the manager to which I referred to earlier in this section. The staff of this manager would spend sometimes 20% of the working time collective "safety evidence" in an attempt to safe guard their positions knowing that if things even went wrong their manager would be the last person to support them and this time was just very obviously wasted and had they had supporting management they would have been doing much more productive things with their time.

Sometimes how the manage reacts is largely driven by the culture of the firm. It can be guaranteed that if you're working for a very old fashioned company then the actions of the management of that firm will mirror the culture, not to do so would in fact be changing the culture itself anyway and the same applies to progressive management. Sometimes this can be an effect of the country which the manager is from, since different countries specialise in different industries just as people do and countries such as European Countries have older more established industries dominating and therefore it would be expected that the style of management there would be more traditional than say West Coast USA where the industries are more of the modern era. This is easily observed in practice where I've worked in Australia where the culture of the organisations follow the West Coast USA quite closely, not so much for the economic reasons of similar industries but more for cultural reasons that the lifestyle and country observes. Manager often are shunted there from the UK by USA firms thinking that the UK and Australia must because close because their political backgrounds are related only to find that the UK manager is a total disaster because the Australia staff find them to be almost fascist. The manager is seen by the Australia staff at best as "touch" and at work as "crazy", "out of touch", "authoritarian" and so staff turnover very quickly accelerates often out of control in a mobile work force environment like Australia has and things only get better once that manager has gone and somebody else put into the place. Had the manager been sent from the West Coast USA, dare say the chance of success would have been very much higher.

With a supportive manager then you should find that your boss will act more as a mentor, somebody to help you progress as your doing the work for the firm and helping the boss progress in their career also. When this happens we get that great win/win scenario where the firm benefits from the increased productivity of the staff, the manager progresses because he's seen to be competent and achieving results and the staff are progressing through learning new shills and progressing in the own development. Unfortunately, I have never seen this situation except in just a few cases with managers that we just outstanding manager and in reality there are very of those in the work force. Most people are practitioners of some type of skill and these skills grow with time, but eventually a point is reached in the 10-20 years after starting work time frame where there's no career progression left being a practitioner of something in which case many are forced into management in order to further their careers. Some make this transition successfully, some not, some become truly great managers, some become simply practitioner in charge of some people, in fact, most are the latter, but no matter which category your boss falls into, they can have a profound effect on your career, your personal development and daily feeling you have towards coming to work.

Manager or Decision Maker / Participative or Autocratic

For manager managers the whole issue of decision making is a major issue, deciding whether to decide or delegate can be a real issue for many managers and they have trouble with this every day. Some manager simply fall back on what they're comfortable with, delegating everything or making every decision for themselves as the case may be but the real skill of being a manager is deciding when a decision should be delegated and when it should simply be made, announced and implemented but many manager can never come to grips with this because they're not really managers, they practitioners in charge of a number of people in the work place.

There are many courses run by the management consulting firms that talk about decision making, they often talk about different management types but they rarely talk about how to decide what the manage should deiced for themselves and what they should be delegating to their staff because this issue is always difficult to solve and often in the real world there's no back and white, right and wrong answer to the issue.

Some managers think that being a manager means they're a leader and as a leader than they're responsible for all the decision making that happens within their realm and while this could be true in the extreme case where the firm is a type of very structured and old fashioned environment it's definitely not the case where the staff are professionals and each has their own growth needs from the position that they're currently working in. People that operate in this manner are not manager but decision makers for other because one of the fundamental skills of managing people is to encourage them to perform to the best of their abilities and to help them to progress with the skills and their usefulness to the firm that they're working for. A "Manager" who blindly makes all the decisions don to small detail is in effect not fulfilling an important part of their job when it comes to the use and development of their staff, but it's surprising how many ":Managers" fall into this trap. It's especially common amongst people that have recently been promoted to be managers for very first time in their lives. It's almost that the allocation of power to them has gone to their heads and they feel as though they need to running and controlling everything around them, much to the total distraction of their staff. For the new manager there are number of fundamental flaws that they commonly fall into:

1. Decision making down to small granularity due to their recent past experience at working at this level
2. Extreme control of staff
3. Telling staff how to do something rather than what needs to be done
4. Autocratic Management style
5. Having "favourite" staff that are like themselves
6. Hiring staff that will become "favourites" because they're like themselves
7. Attempt to remove staff that they haven't personally selected because they're concerned about their degree of loyalty to the new manager

I have seen one newly appointed manager fall into every single one of these traps and as a result, he earned the condemnation of everyone around him. He managed to hold his position for about 18 months and then left gracefully before being pushed. But many other new managers will inadvertently fall into several of these traits through their own inexperience and whole some firms realise that this is all part of the learning experience for the new manager the transition period while the new manager can learn these skills can be chaotic for the firm in terms of staff turnover.

Of course the other extreme is the manager who is scared to make decisions at all and so they tend to delegate everything to their staff. This is a kind of way of "opting out" f the responsibility for the resulting decision that was made, at least that's what the manager thinks because they can always blame others, but it misses the obvious point that the manager is till responsible for the actions of their own group regardless of who makes the actual decision, the decision to move ahead with the decision is ultimately that of the manager who bears the final responsibility for the results, be they good or bad for the firm.

What really needs to be considered by the manager when it comes to the making of decisions is that they need to undertake bearing in mind the staff that you're working with, the type of decision, whether it's very structured or not, he resulting impact it will have on the firm and the amount of information available to the decision makers at the critical point in time at which the decision is made. Anything on the more structured, high impact end of the spectrum is best decided by the manager, especially if expediency is a factor, while other decisions can be delegated to staff or made jointly with the manager acting as a facilitator.

All this is fine in real life, it's a case of what should be happening, but the reality of the situation is that most manager stay with what they're comfortable with, making decisions or avoiding them.

Cannon Fodder

One thing that many younger workers need to watch out for & be aware of is the fact that some managers aren't adverse to the use of "Cannon Fodder" in the work place to cover their own problems or to create a scape goat to find others to blame. Managers from the UK are particularly susceptible to this tactic to cover their mistakes & I think a lot of this comes back to the "quaint" old English Class traditions where the upper class can do whatever they like to the lower class & this translates directly into action in the work place, where the manger assumes the higher class status & they feel free to make sacrifices to save their own problems as the need may arise. Although I find this prevalent in managers from the UK I have seen it used in other places too & for the newcomer to the workforce it can be catastrophic for their early career advancement if they're in the wrong place at the wrong time with a ruthless manager who uses this practice. The new employee thinks that they're being given a great opportunity to prove themselves when in reality they've been put into a position from which they can never achieve a positive result, nor were they ever meant to, because the manager in question expects to use them as the excuse for things going wrong & in the worst cases fire them on that basis, showing the firm that the manager has the firm hand that's needed at times to remove an "incompetent" employee when the need arises. I know of one manager in particular that uses this to effect & yes, this manager is from the UK. There was one incident where the customer had asked for staff with five years experience in a particular field, but the firm had been operating in that country only for about three years. The manager told the customer that the best he could do was three years experience which the customer accepted. The problem for the manager as that he had already sold this three years experience resource into several sites already because all the rest of the staff were very new to the firm. The manager picked a new employee & gave him instruction that he was to take the place of the three years experience staff member & that it was his problem to deal with the issue after that. When the time came to introduce the new staff member to the client, the manager made sure he was on an overseas trip & left the duties to another third party who had no knowledge of what had transpired so far. Needless to say, the customer kept asking for the experienced staff member that was promised & of course he was never forthcoming. The customer felt if they complained about the new staff member then the promised three years experienced resource promised to surface, so they complained violently & the new staff member, knowing he was the manager's scape goat transferred to another group within the firm before things went too far. In this case the employee was shrewd enough to know what was happening, but to recap, the manager deliberately lied to a customer & then threw a new staff member into the fire with the intention of firing him at a later date in order to buy time to attempt to find some more experienced resources elsewhere in the world to fill the need. After this, the manager in question was promoted to Director in recognition of his "special" contributions to the firm!

This was a rather extreme case of the use of "Cannon Fodder", but in lesser cases you can actually turn this bad situation into something good for you, because if you're in the situation where there's any chance at all of achieving a success, then if you can do this, even partially, you'll earn enormous respect of your manager & of those around you. Many in the firm will know that you were "thrown to the wolves" & somehow through your own efforts managed to survive. If you can survive this, then you'll have set an impression that will be difficult to fault from that time onwards, but to arrive at this point will be extremely difficult.

How Did My Boss Become the Boss?

There are many ways that the boss can become the boss and the most common which most management and especially HR books don't like to talk about is seniority. It's not popular or trendy to say that, but it's true that seniority is still probably the single most important determinate in where you'll be placed in the firms hierarchy and I mean seniority in the number of years you've been working since you started work since these days nobody expects (or necessarily wants) staff to have stayed in the same firm their entire working career. Think about what you see when you read position descriptions, one thing you'll never miss is an "indicative" number of years of work experience that would be required to undertake the position and while it may be marked as "indicative" what the HR managers are thinking in the back of their minds as they're sifting through the applications is "has this person worked for enough years" if "yes", then your application will proceed through the process, if "no" you receive the "thanks but no thanks" letter for the firm in a few weeks time. While there might be exception to what I've just described the exceptions then to be very few and then tend to be those of companies run by younger people themselves that have been successful by starting their own business' or by those attempting to give a "young image' to their company, but the real truth is that seniority is responsible in the very vast majority of cases for your appointment or not to any given position. Even perfect qualifications and 100% totally relevant job experience can only make a finite amount of head way against experience and in response to this I've seen colleagues doing things like dying their hair grey on their temples so that they can look five years older! Thinking that this would help them get the positions and some are absolutely adamant that this did in fact help on occasion. I find it interesting to hear older people saying they're on the scarp heap of workers because of their age and I wonder if this really is the case, I would suspect that this is only partly true and I would also suspect that part of the problem is that many older workers have older skills that are simply not in demand anymore and because of this they're dislocated employment wise, because they want to work, but their skill set is obsolete and therefore they can't work because they're no in demand anymore and the effects of globalisation tends to hasten this effect rather than prevent it.

In the Public Sector this effect of seniority is even more pronounced and while there has been a great focus on this in past years the truth is that it really hasn't changed very much because in lots of countries the Public Sector is a type of bastion of Unionism which simply won't let the rules of the past be change quickly. In this type of environment there is little incentive to work much harder than your colleagues because the principle of seniority will stifle you opportunity to climb the ladder and so things tend to gravitate towards a "norm" based on more or less the lowest common denominator within sensible reason. Mind you, this not need always be a bad thing and in the past 20 years or so there's been a lot of debate about the Public Sector on various countries and there's issues to consider such as some people are willing and will very much prefer to receive some less money than thy could earn elsewhere and in return they're happier to work in more secure surroundings with little risk of retrenchment or layoff and not to have to feel the pressure of the "profit motive". Being a manager in this type of environment means being able to precisely split up work loads and allocate to staff, teach staff what they need to know to be able to do the job and also, not make too many big decisions yourself because if you make big and risky decisions you might get something wrong and upset others who you have to work with every day beyond today. You'd also tend to make all the decisions regarding your department yourself since you'd expect your staff not to be too interested or enthusiastic to make too many decisions of their own. While this does conjure images of the Public Sector being slow, old fashioned and behind in the ways that management thinks and acts, as a generalization it's true and it's one of the main reasons that many Governments have gone towards privatisation over the past 15 years or so. The Governments on a number of political fronts haven't been able to change this very much because the senior staff of many Government organisations have something of a contempt for the politicians. They seen them as people who will be there for one or two elected terms but the staff of the Government Department are there forever and so many politicians have vainly tried to change the Public Sector with no real outcomes to speak of since their tendency is to simply ignore politicians and their programmes and do the absolute minimum necessary in their efforts towards changing things.

In the private sector you'll find many more variation on the theme when it comes to the issue of how your boss or manager got to the position to which they're currently at. There's almost no doubt that seniority will have some effect on the outcomes but there will also be issues more surrounding the types of experience that the manager has had rather than the absolute number of years and it becomes a type balance of seniority in the direct and absolute relevant job experience combined to a degree with the absolute number of working years that the manager has worked that becomes the determinate. In any event the private sector will usually more fully consider directly relevant work experience since the Public Service has a tendency to think in terms of very high level generic skill sets and attempts to classify very diverse workers skill sets into these classes, while the Private Sector very much more understands specialization, although there are still places where this is not fully understood.

Mentor

Some manager take on the role o mentor for their newer staff member and this can have great effect to the firm with regard to the personal development of the newer staff members. I worked for one firm where there was an official mentor program and in this program it was not your boss, but somebody in your own group that was more senior to yourself that was assigned to be your mentor. There was even a half day course run which explained what the firm was hoping to achieve and how it would be implemented and at first it al appeared to be take very seriously, but the whole thing failed and fell apart in the end. The reasons being that this firm was a consulting firm and the staff were traveling all the time and thy never got the chance to meet to discuss things and he mentors themselves being the more senior staff had very high targets to meet with regard to bringing in revenue and so they never really had the tie to spare to run the scheme efficiently or properly. So while at first this scheme appeared to have a lot of promise for the newer staff members it wasn't implemented so well and the daily needs to get things done again over run the long term benefits.

Being a mentor is one of those tasks that manager managers don't even really think should be their task to perform. Many see their roles as decision maker and budget manager and nothing much beyond these tasks, but it's the extra tasks like being a mentor to the more junior staff that truly makes the difference between a good manager and an ordinary one. Some manager just naturally have the people skills to enable them to do things like the mentor role well, but other just don't have those types of skills and those that don't would even argue as to them needing to perform that type of role anyway. If you're new to the work place if you can somehow identify that a prospective employer will act in this mentor manner then you'll be very lucky as this will allow you to grow career wise in your position much fast than for somebody that has to find out all everything the hard way by themselves through their own trial and error.

It could be that you prospective mentor could even be outside the organisation in which you work, but they could be inside you industry, so for many more junior staff it's good to become member of professional organisation and mix with those more experienced. I know myself these can be boring and stuffy affairs to attend but just occasionally you can meet somebody who really is an outstanding individual in their chosen career path. The ability of a mentor to help can be an amazing boost to your career prospects, even if it's just somebody else that works in the same sphere as yourself but they have five or more years more experience than you do yourself. The insights that such a person can have to help you can put you years ahead of your colleagues over time as your career progresses.

Manager's Motivating their Staff

The manager is also responsible for trying to motivate their staff and while this is not easy during difficult times for the firm it does not abrogate the manager from this responsibility.

There are many ways that the manager can affect the motivation of their staff and some of these ways can have good effect while other can be bad and some catastrophic. Many managers often forget about this part of their role because they're often very task oriented, which is fine because many firms have task oriented HR policies and bonus policies, but in their zeal to pursue the short term objectives of performance the long term role of motivating their staff can often be forgotten about in the rush to do so many other things.

Much of the motivation of the employee has to do with expectation, not only of what the manager expects from them in the way of work output, but also expectation of what the job role is and how it is to be done. Manager managers go wrong right from the point of undertaking the job interview in that they set the expectations wrongly, be it deliberately which you'd be surprised how often that occurs or more often the case, inadvertently. The manage will be conducting the interview bearing in mind that they want the best possible person and when doing the interviews although most interview techniques say reserve your decision until the end, the manager will often decide in their own minds which individual is right for the position and from that point they'll start to attempt to talk you into accepting the position and it's at this point that the expectation setting can go off the rails. The manager will be attempting to portray the position in such a way that the staff member will see the position as attractive and as being a good piece of experience in the own career progression and this portrayal could in fact not be 100% genuine and in many cases it's not because that manager is trying to entice you to accept the position. Once you accepted the position and joined the company then the power axis shifts to the manager who is now fully in control and you can find that what you accepted isn't really 100% the reality of the situation, but you've left your old position and therefore it's not likely you'll go back. Many managers rely on this strategy to entice the staff that they really want and while it may sound strange to say the manager will entice the staff this really is the case once the manager has mentally made the decision which staff member they want to hire. Think about how we but things, you make your decision to buy on sometimes superfluous things like colour or aesthetics, then once you've made that decision you look for reasons to justify that purchase. I think this is the case very much more often than sitting down and quantitatively evaluating all of the factors that would sensibly be in consideration which would then lead you to an outcome. I really do think it's a case of the potential employee holding the power prior to accepting the offered position and leaving their old company, but once that happens the power base shifts. I myself have learned to be quite tough when negotiating new positions, for me now, the position has to be right, the title has to be right and the remuneration has to be right otherwise it's not on and while this would of course limit the number o positions I would be accepted for, when I do get accepted my motivation never suffers because I've always made the deal bearing that in mind. If you make too many compromises in this phase your motivation will suffer at a later date.

The other major effect that your manager can have on motivation is how much they will let you grow. Many managers will simply not let their staff grow too much because they're always conscious that the staff member showing too much initiative may become a potential replacement for themselves over time. The more junior staff member may progress to the point where they can substituted into the manager role with a lower salary and so in those difficult times when cost cutting is going on then that great staff member may in fact become a threat and so many manager will attempt to limit the growth of such individuals by making sure that they don't get the roles and work that would allow them to progress. The manager knows that over time the staff member will have problems with their motivation and will ultimately leave, thereby securing their position. This can of course work the other way around when the manager perceives the excellent staff member as a friend and ally in which case the reverse can apply and the manager can groom the staff member for promotion maybe to another area, but in those circumstances there's that unique and rare win/win situation that's often not seen too much in the real world.

What ever approach the manager decides to take, motivating their staff is a task that's very important to the long term performance of the organisation and although there's always the tendency for the short term needs to overcome the long term needs just to get things done every day, the long term issue of motivation is very important to the performance of the firm, the manager's own personal results in the longer term and the morale and growth of the staff members.

Follow Your Boss Up The Ladder

One of the simplest and quickest methods of climbing up the ladder is to follow your boss up the ladder if you've correctly identified that he's a mover up the corporate ladder. I've seen this happen on a few occasions and sometimes the following by the staff member has been totally accidental but other times it was quite deliberate but the result was the same, promotion and progress for both the manager and their immediate subordinate with very little effort being expended by the subordinate. The logic of this is that if you boss moves up the ladder, the old hole left by your boss' move up would most logically be filled by yourself. Because you and your boss have a great rapport then if you do have difficulty fulfilling the role then your boss can mentor you and help you grow into the role as he's doing the same. If you're really lucky and your boss can progress again, then the whole process can repeat itself, but here's usually limits on ho many levels you can climb the ladder using this method.

The absolutely critical thing that has to be in place for this to work for you is that you have to be totally confident that your boss sees you as a friend and ally, somebody that they can trust to help them when things are difficult and at the same time you have to absolutely sure that you're the only one that you boss regards in this manner otherwise it may not work for you, somebody else may get the chance to follow your boss up the ladder instead.

The other thing that's essential for this to work is that your boss has to have been brought in from outside the existing structure of the firm with some type of mandate from the very top of the organisation to change things. Remember, that the HR policies of the firm will be working against you to advance quickly both in term of position and salary, they'll be trying to "pigeon hole" you into your slot from which it's difficult to move over time and it's only that mandate from the top that can work effectively against that. That mandate to change things is the only way that you can present the argument that the normal rules don't need to apply to yourself o your boss and as a result these types of situations don't occur very frequently in real life very often. In fact, they are so rare that it's never happened to myself but I have seen it happen only twice in organisations in which I've worked but I've been too distant from the manager and the operations role of that manager in question to work it myself.

The one thing to remember about this way to advance is that the mandate to change things doesn't ever last forever. It's usually short term over the course of a few years at the very most and so you have to take full advantage of that few years because it's going to be a long term thing. Most change managers are there with a few specific tasks to perform and once that's been done and the whole thing bedded down successfully then that manager will move on because typically the cost of these types of change activities to the firm are very high, so the top management of the firm are always watching to keep the cost of such activities to a minimum both in cost but also minimising the time for which this changing period will occur. As a result this approach can easily get you to be promote once up the ladder, sometimes twice if you're very lucky but it's not likely to get you a third promotion because this will start to raise the ire of others in the firm, in fact, even a second promotion in the course of less than to years will generally unsettle others around you to the point where action will be done to prevent any further increases in role and status in the short term. There's always the "Tall Poppy Syndrome" that will be active to prevent further advancement for anyone working this way, both for the boss whose using their mandate to change to move up the ladder but also for yourself. Many will become envious when they see what's happening and start to ask question surrounding what's happening in an attempt to prevent further increases in salary and status for yourself and your boss.

In the two real life cases where I saw this happen myself the upper management that gave the initial mandate for change put an end to the change practices because staff turnover had increased after some staff had felt that the manager in question and his subordinate had in effect been promoted over the heads of other "more deserving" (due to the reasons of seniority) other staff. Some of the resignations had actually cited this as a contributing reason for them leaving, in order to gain the type of promotion that they'd been working towards for years without success in the firm elsewhere. After this happened the manager in question left the organisation to pursue change management opportunities at another firm in the same industry, the subordinate was left behind in his much elevated position but this person did not receive any cooperation from other staff and managers who felt he hadn't earned the position. He eventually left and pursued a similar position with another firm where because he was hired on at that same level and none of those issues presented themselves again because the history of his rise was in effect left behind. So while this method can get you ahead quickly and easily compared with other methods it does have it associated longer term dangers for you to consider.

Budget

For most managers it's the budget that's the real key to their ability to succeed if that's ever going to happen. Many managers complain that they actually spend the bulk of their time arguing for money from their firm in order to be allowed to do the job that they're supposed to be doing and the sheer fact that they spend all this time arguing for the very money that they need to run things is the thing hindering their ability to succeed in the longer term. The other thing to remember is that the manager's ability to gain the funding required to manage their departments also has an effect on their ability to give pay increments to their staff, so in a very strong and rigid way, a way in which you can have very little effect in the process, your ability for increased earning power of time is very closely linked to your boss' ability to argue effectively from the firm for the funding to keep their department running. This is very unfortunate in a lot of cases but it's one of those harsh realities that you have to face and have to work with. Of course this means that you should be doing everything you can to assist your boss perform that argument for increased funding, but in most cases, it's something you won't even know is happening until it's all over and the outcomes is decided and for those of us that are lucky to work for managers that are very effective at this process be it due to their natural or learned abilities then we can expect some good increments over time, but then for those of us working for those managers that are more task oriented, who prefer to get on with the direct work and not sped the time necessary to gain funding from the management of the firm, then we can expect our departments that we work for to become less funded over time and out own pay increments to become less funded over time. Eventually there will be a point where the manager is actually so ineffective, not due to their own personal lack of skill, but to lack of available resources that they will either leave themselves and the firm will perform some kind of restructure around what's been happening or you'll just keep suffering.

The only respite from this situation would be in the larger firms where the pay scales are equated with each other, such as firms using formal HR systems where at least you'll be assured o some kind of pay increment, although these very rigid HR systems in some environments can be more a hindrance than a help to the developments of the staff in the firm and for the staff themselves in the pursuit of salary increases based on learned skills and marketability rather than sheer budget increase. This of course handles the payroll case but it does nothing to address the situation where a single department of affirm may be "strangled" to death because they don't have the funding necessary to do anything.

Employee Motivation

Happy Staff are Productive Staff?

It's often been said that Happy Staff are Productive staff, but is this really true? A lot of companies think that if people are too happy then maybe they're not being pushed enough to work hard for the firm and there is evidence to support this.

Some manager's feel that they have to push their staff to work and some feel that their staff are motivated enough to work by themselves with only direction setting being required. There are many schools of thought on this issue and there's all kind of approaches that are undertaken in the working environment. A lot of management theories follow the line that if the tasks are very structured then pushing the staff will be required and that less structured tasks that require the use of individual thought will be staffed by much more professional staff who will require very minimal supervision. It has been my observation that this is quite correct.

The time when this all falls to the ground is when there is personality clashes in the workforce. Most companies don't cope with this situation well at all. What can you do when you and your boss don't get along? What can you do when you find that your boss' boss appointed your boss in the first place and therefore has a vested interest in making sure that the person they personally selected is seen to be successful because a failure may reflect on them? In these circumstances then the normal reaction in the company is for everyone to pretend there's not a problem and wait for something to happen. It is then expected that the aggrieved employee to try and find another job and leave the organisation typically.

Some companies have periodic surveys in an attempt to gauge the "happiness" of the staff and I've seen one company in particular go to great length to conduct surveys and analyse the result. At first the employees were cynical that the results would actually lead to any change and of course they were right. Plenty of statistics were collected and the major problem areas identified with the reasoning that lots of problems couldn't be solved at once, but a few at a time could be solved and over time things would get better, quite good logic I think, but the problems was that the areas identified by the staff related to two managers in particular and some of the more politically controversial issues in the organisation, so the management decided to move down the list, in doing so, they completely undermined the whole result of the survey and the staff knew this very well. At the time it was all considered too hard to tackle the real problems and because of this the staff weren't happy, morale suffered, people started to leave the organisation and the staff weren't really as productive as they could have been.

Team building is also another method that is used by managers to attempt to build a team spirit and make staff happy as a unit to function together. I've seen mixed results here with some team building exercises ending in disaster like the time staff were asked to swing from branches of trees 50 feet above the ground in order to build trust between them, but it didn't build much trust in the over weight middle aged lady who spent two years receiving worker's compensation insurance from her broken and dislocated bones. At the same time I've seen really simple things like a few trips to the bar after work and a few dinners with the right group of people that really appreciate that type of thing work wonders for team spirit. The moral of the story here is that team building exercises can really work wonders for staff morale, but you have to be very careful what the type of exercise is, some of the more exotic and elaborate schemes are viewed very cynically by the staff and some of the more basic simple things can be really appreciated and have an overwhelming positive effect.

So while the old "Happy Employees are Productive Employees" is generally correct there are some practical considerations to think about when it comes to the implementation in the work place.

Turnover

Turnover is a big issue for some firms, especially because the cost of introducing new staff to the firm can be very high. The costs can mount up because there's recruitment costs, training costs and the simple cost of lost productivity because the new staff member will take some time to "come up to speed" to the point where they're as productive as the old staff member who left. If staff turnover is so expensive then why is it allowed to happen? There are a number of factors to consider when considering the answer to this question.

Lack of career planning is a major issue for most firms leading to staff turnover. Most firms provide no clear direction to their staff as to where they might progress over time despite what their HR Department might say about the use of career planning activities. The employee feels that they're not likely to progress in their career feeling that their longer term aspiration are not likely to be met. As a result a move to another organisation in order to take up a new position consistent with the staff member's desire for career progression is seen as the best option for the staff member. This can also be the case where the employee has a high need for progression and learning in the type of work they do. Employees that have a high need for learning in the work place

Personality clash issues can contribute to staff turnover as described in the previous section of this chapter. It's only once this has become truly serious that most companies will act to remove the manager from the line of command. One, two or three people leaving is not normally enough, it takes truly high staff turnover before a manager will be recognised as the problem contributing to staff turnover, but large turnover in one area of the firm is a classic indicator that the manager in question can't cope with the "People" side of the position & in my opinion should immediately raise the attention of the management of the firm, since experienced people are hard to retain & give a lot to the firm, no firm wants to leave good people because an individual manager can't perform the people side of the role, but I have seen this happen all too often, it's actually very common in the real world.

Salary issues can also cause staff turnover, especially when salary rises are not consistent with the external environment. This is also a double problem for those firms facing financial difficulty because they can ill afford to face the costs of recruitment of new staff and so the salary issues can in fact become more of an issue quickly if staff decide en masse to leave over these kinds of issues.

Redundancy is also another major factor contributing to staff turnover because once somebody is made redundant in most companies then everyone else around them starts to feel uneasy and people start to look for other alternatives and once they start to look around then some will find greener pastures and make the move to leave the company. It's for this reason that companies must think carefully about their long term existence before deciding to make staff redundant. Those with the best, newest and most mobile job skills will be the ones that can find their greener pastures and once some people decide to move, then word spreads internally that greener pastures exist and then more staff leave, the whole process can become self sustaining.

Training

Training is a big problem for most companies because it's a double cost, it's a cost to do the training and invest money in an individual that might leave the organisation taking the investment with them one day, but it's also the cost of the lost productivity of staff member not being on site to do their usual work. It's with this in mind that most employers approach the issue of training on the job.

In most companies training falls victim to the short term mentality. Because of its long term nature, training is often one of the very first things that is cut when times are busy or budgets are strained and while this may not have much effect in the short term, continual deferment can be an issue for both staff and the firm. For the individual it means job skills slowly decline and become obsolete, resulting in decreased job mobility in the longer term. For those with this in mind and for those with high internal needs to learn, this may increase the staff turnover rate as some staff conscious of their declining skills move onto greener pastures. For the firm, continual declining and obsolescence of job skills means less effective staff over time which is a very serious long term issue. It can be addressed only by introduction of newer staff with the required skills at that later point in time, presumably at a premium cost or large retaining programs at a later time, when the firm may be just as unable to absorb the temporary diversion of staff and costs as they are now.

Another issue with training is that some specialised training is that it may actually lead to staff losses. A good example is that ERP and CRM software packages are very much in favour and there is a shortage of staff with experience with these systems and in these fields, even having training in some of the major packages can greatly increase the staff member's job mobility. Some companies face the issue where they have bought and implemented these types of systems and training staff will mean that they can now qualify for jobs at other companies paying 20-70% higher and so staff loss is almost a certainty under these circumstances. When faced with this situation it may come as no surprise that some companies choose to deliberately not train their staff to save the cost of the training, the short term loss of productivity and the likely loss of staff.

The same applies to university studies, many managers accept the fact that their staff undertaking part time college or university studies will almost certainly leave the organisation at or near the completion of their studies because they know they simply won't be allows by the HR Department to make a salary offer at any kind of level to keep that staff member. This is because most companies do not employ any sensible career planning of any type. For this reason many companies do nothing to encourage continuing college or university studies for their staff because it's perceived by the firm as the employee undertaking a long term strategy to skill up and leave the organisation to receive better money elsewhere at a later date

Because of the issues noted here what ends up happening in most companies with regard to training is that they put on some very generic training that can be held in large classes in order to be seen to be doing the right thing, to be providing training for their staff, without actually giving the staff skills that might increase their job mobility and without costing very much, such as the traditional Presentation Skill and Negotiating Skills courses that are held by many training and consulting firms.

So although training is a vital issue to most employees, my general observation is that it is generally handled very badly in industry. The smart employee has to remember that their skills are the key to their income and continued employment. It's not likely that the employer will make any kind of long term serious attempt to keep your skills up to date, in fact the reverse will be true over a period of time. So it's very important that you keep yourself skilled up with current useful in demand skills, even if you have to pay yourself for the courses. The best way to think of it is that it's like any other investment where you put money in, in the first instance but you'll reap the returns in the longer term. Those who fail to realise that they own their own skills and the maintenance of their own skills is the key to their livelihood are those that tend to find themselves in the unemployment queues, with little prospect of finding work due to outdated and obsolete skill sets.

The Annual Performance Review

Of everything I've discussed in this paperback regarding motivation and reward for the employee, this would have to be the worst implemented aspect of anything ever implemented wide scale in the work force. I've read many management books that say words to the effect that the Annual Performance Review should be used as an opportunity to provide positive reinforcement for the employee, to reward performance, to set direction and provide a framework to ensure that the employee is motivated to perform over the next performance review period, but in reality nothing could be further from the truth, in fact, as implemented in most organised the complete and exact reverse is generally true. Many organisation brag about how effectively this process works, how their staff are motivated by the process and that staff are rewarded based on the Annual Performance Review results and while this may be true to some extent there are very strict limits to how true this really is in most organisations and some organisations are just simply lying when they say this, but they say this because they feel that in today's dynamic world you should be saying and doing this. Not being seen to be participating is as if admitting you're doing something wrong and we can never admit we're doing something wrong or we might lose face – right?

Another issue with this process is the actually time to perform this process. Many managers are loaded heavily with their daily activities and so performing the Annual Review Processes something which they feel impinges on their daily activities. It's with this in the back of their minds that many manager walk into the Annual Performance Review session.

Performance appraisals generally have some type of objectives that have been set and your performance will be measured against this criteria. Often though, the performance criteria have become irrelevant over the course of the past year, but the HR Department insists on quantitative assessment, which means you're assessed against objectives that aren't relevant. The other thing that happens is that the objectives weren't relevant to the employee in the very first place because the manager last year didn't have enough time available amongst their other duties to ensure that the employee received relevant and individual objectives, but again the HR insists on quantitative assessments.

When you are assessed there's often a scale that the results are ranked against, like from one to five with for example being one means terrible or non performance, three is average and five is totally outstanding, but the problem with this is that extreme scores require explanation so many manager are very reluctant to give extreme scores even when they are deserved, so the tendency is to give everyone average scores. The result of this is that there is a stifling of outstanding performance and lower than average performance is allowed to continue indefinitely.

Also there's often some generic criteria for assessment, well, more generic than the actually objectives in themselves in most organisations that are intended to reflect the core values of the organisation itself, but these items are usually scored in much the same way as for the objectives, very generically with extreme scores requiring management explanation with the same outcomes as for the objectives, incentive stifled and below average performance rewarded.

Eventually when you get to the end of this process the results are purely subjective, so if you and your boss are on really good terms you're really lucky and if this isn't the case then you better start to look for a new job. In fact I've seen one "manager" use this process as poor excuse to invoke a "Personal Improvement Plan" for individuals that he didn't personally like and once this was invoked then the implication was you better start to look for a new job because there was no possible redemption. After all, in the case of disputes will your organisation support you, or your boss? Especially when your boss' boss has often appointed your boss and has a vested interest in supporting your boss. Only repeated issues regarding the same manager over a prolonged period of time will give you any chance to survive any adverse issues and even then, it won't be easy.

Then, with the result to the Annual Review Process completed your pay rise, if any is determined, well, that's the theory, but in reality the Budget for next year has already been decided and that's the cap on your potential rise and if the Budget has been held anything close to frozen still then you're pay rise won't be much, despite any performance. This is related very much on the section where I discuss the old adage "You Have to Spend Money to Make Money", but the setting of the budget is the single most important facto to your potential pay rise. The idea that your performance has any major impact is purely illusionary in most organisations.

Many firm's HR Departments really cannot and never will come to grips wit the concept that a highly skilled and specialised subordinate could be more valuable in the workforce than their manager. So out in the open work force a worker with a very high demand skill set could easily command a salary premium that is higher than the open market rate for their manager who ha a more generic skill set. Many firms will never recognise this and so the more skilled the subordinate is, the more likely they will leave as time goes along.

The employees approach to the Review also has little effect on the outcomes too. I've seen aggressive people going in ready to attack their boss who might not have such a strong personality, thinking they can walk over their boss to a large pay rise and I've seen people walk meekly in, hoping their boss will be kind and every shade of grey in between, but the outcomes have never really been any different in the way or pay rise and promotional prospects, the only difference is the anger level of the individuals involved. Going in with a reason argument why you deserve a pay rise is the most often suggested approach in the text books and while I have experienced this being successful occasionally, the sad reality is that most people achieve their best pay rises by using the skills learned to take to another employer and gain a rise at the same time as they change jobs.

In any event the use of the Annual Performance Review in most organisation is a complete waste of time which accomplishes nothing other than waste people's time and everyone involved is made to play a ridiculous game of charades in order to keep the HR Department happy that the system is being implemented correctly and of course because it's being implemented correctly then it must be working. The reality is the Annual Performance Review process in most organisations is designed to provide a shield that the manager's can hide behind in order to justify not giving pay rises on behalf of the firm, pay rises they may really want to give, but are unable because of the budgetary limits. I have seen so many attempts to try and do this in organisations, in scores of companies and I have never once anywhere in any country seen anything even close to resembling a sensible and honest approach to the Annual Performance Review. The Annual Performance Review seems to be the single major item that brings out the very worst elements in everyone involved and in a lot of companies is a major source of employee dissatisfaction and resentment.

The Personal Development Plan

The Personal Development Plan is another area of continues failure for most HR Departments in industry. Like most initiatives of the HR kind, the motives are noble and well intentioned but the execution leaves a lotto be desired in most companies. Again HR falls victim to being viewed by higher management as an overhead to be minimized and as a result there is usually insufficient resources allocated to undertake this process properly in most organisations.

Done properly we would expect to see the Personal Development Plan used as a guide to determine the strengths and weaknesses of the employee and then an attempt to work on the weaknesses and build on the strengths. Also a definition of what skills the employee would be expected to gain over time would be defined and a plan put in place to allow the employee to achieve this outcome would be put into place. This would of course be undertaken in conjunction with career and succession planning exercises to determine who would be the best fits to different positions over time and give the employee a sense of direction, belonging to the organisation and a sense of feeling achievement and advancement over time, but having said this, these ideal circumstances are almost never realised in practice.

In reality, what usually happens is that because of time constraints with the employee's manager, resource constraints in the HR department and budget constraints with regard to the use of training, the whole exercise ends up becoming a useless pen pushing exercise if in fact it is done at all and many organisations don't do this at all. The outcome and usefulness of this is usually similar to the outcomes of the Annual Performance Review. To quote myself in an earlier passage: "everyone involved is made to play a ridiculous game of charades".

Remuneration

One of the most controversial aspects of employment in almost all organisations is that of remuneration.

Not only is there the basic amount that the employee is paid but also the break down of how it is structured and the effect that this has to the employees motivation that results from this absolute figure paid and it's structure. Also there is tendency for the employees to make strong comparison with their colleagues concerning remuneration and inconsistency and inequity based on the employees own set of values when making the comparison can be the cause of discontent. This is the challenge for the employer because the employer is not always able to just the basis of the set of core values that the employee will be using when making these comparisons.

One important thing to remember for most people in most organisations when it comes to the issue of remuneration is that the point at which you enter an organisation is VERY important to your level of payment. In most organisations it's been my observation that at the point at which you take your new job and enter the organisation defines your pay scale, irrespective if whether you're promoted over time and irrespective of the increase in your responsibility, process ownership and technical knowledge. There are simple very finite limits on how much a firm will increase an individual's pay each year and it's for this reason that nearly all MBA graduates leave their firm upon graduation, it's because the HR and Payroll Policies and the approved budgets won't allow for the employee to make big jumps in pay, in fact these policies are specifically designed to do the reverse, to prevent big jumps in pay. The point that I'm making here is that to advance your remuneration, you really do need to leave your organisation and go to another firm, where you can enter that firm at a higher point than where you currently sit, that is, promotion by changing jobs which I talk at more length in the Changing Jobs section of this book. Be very careful of promises that your remuneration will grow quickly over time as these promises are nearly always not true and are being made at that point in time to get you to accept a position that you may not be fully confident of accepting. If you ask for that promise in writing I'd be very surprised if you get it and a year later nobody will know, remember or even care that such a promise was made. I've seen this done by so many firms over and over again and people are still falling into this trap every single day, taking the firm on it's word but the day never arrives when the firm delivers on it's word because that promise was made without any factual backing of the firm and it's current policies. Another, even more deceitful practice I've seen in the past is the issuing of share options of firms that have not even listed yet on the stock market as substitution for salary. The new employee feels that they can make a fortune in the next few years with the options but the truth is that the firm never intends to list! Always be VERY careful of these two situations !

Another problem, especially with large firms that have very rigid HR and Payroll policies is the structuring of the Remuneration package. Most large companies offer some type of offer that is easy to administer but not necessarily matching the needs and wants of the employee, nor may these packages be structured ideally from a taxation point of view. This lack of flexibility and structure can result in employee dissatisfaction over time and when it comes to evaluating offers from other employers, these factors will be considered by the employee in making that vital "change job": decision.

Another observation of mine is that the medium size firms cope so much better in this area than the large firms. They are small enough to be flexible but large enough to make good salary offers which the large organisation is usually hamstrung by over complex and inefficient HR and payroll rules that are of dubious value. Smaller firms are great for their flexibility but really not able to make top quality salary offers generally.

Redundancy and the Effects on Those Remaining

Redundancy can have a devastating effect on organisations, not only on those who are chosen to be made redundant, but also for the morale of those who remain behind and the culture of the organisation. In many cases the first round of redundancy is the beginning of the end for organisations.

Companies are in the position where their performance is directly related to "Head Count", may of the financial analysts figures are dependant upon the number, such as Sales per Employee, Profit per Employee etc. So there is a direct incentive for most companies to keep their staff numbers as low as is possible at all times, especially at the end of the quarter when stock market reporting is required, because it's at these times when the financial analysts will be digesting the figures reported.

So, in order to keep the financial figures looking as good as possible the company has decided to cull staff. How will this be done? There are numerous possibilities:

One common approach is to attempt to remove those staff that are not directly earning money for the company. This is common in service industry companies because it's easy to identify who does and does not earn money directly for the firm. It's at these times that you see those with high annual salaries and low direct dollar earning effect on the company ducking and hiding and running for cover, HR, IT, Accounting and Engineering managers and their staff are especially susceptible at these times, since many firms view HR and IT especially as overheads that are to be minimized and the managers of these departments are seen as especially superfluous, but culling the IT operational staff maybe have dire effects in the longer term due to the traditionally high mobility of those working is this profession.

Another approach taken in larger organisations is to choose a percentage of staff to cut right across the board, every group in the organisation has to cull the same percentage. While on the surface this would appear to be fair, it's often a way for management to avoid the really hard decisions. This also has the effect that productive staff valuable to the running of the organisation will may be culled as will departments that may already be running lean of staff have their staff numbers cut. In this environment the manager has the opportunity to remove staff that they don't want, with sometimes little reason to why they're not wanted often giving the manager the opportunity to bring in personal feelings into the decision of who to cut, especially in the support parts of the organisation in the departments where the staff do not earn direct external revenue for the firm. This method of staff reduction can often cause as many problems as it solves.

Anyway, once the word "redundancy" is used staff get nervous and when people are actually selected for redundancy, given their severance cheques and sent on their way then silent alarm bells rings throughout the office and silent panic sets in. Silent panic then causes the staff to start to look around for other jobs, because the group mentality is to get out while the going is still good because everyone wants to avoid the pain of being made redundant. The longer the process of staff cuts go on, the longer staff are looking around for other work and what starts to happen over time is that the loss of staff becomes self feeding, some staff go through the redundancy process through whatever selection method but then other staff start to leave of their own accord. The issue for the firm is that the staff that leave of their own accord are not those selected by the management of the firm, in fact they're the ones with the best job skills in the most mobile market segments and what happens over times is knowledge vacuums starts to appear because the most knowledgeable and valuable staff with the best job skills are the ones that are the first to leave under these circumstances. In extreme circumstances I've seen whole departments almost cease to exist because of this type of staff loss with the resulting chaos to the organisation as they attempt then to rebuild what has been lost and included in this rebuilding chaos is the high cost of training and induction of new people, so the cost to the firm can in fact be quite high if the redundancy process is not handled well.

There are possibilities for advancement in such circumstances for the individual however. For those with the nerves of steel to stay behind and not leave the firm, there maybe promotional opportunities to take the places of those who leave. Again the ones who can take this strategy are those with the best job skills, since this course may backfire with the department maybe being outsourced if things are really that bad. If you're confident of your job skills and mobility then this can be a good course of action, but not so for those without the nerves, the skill and the mobility.

Changing Jobs

Why Would You Do It?

For many people changing their employer is a really big step, so it begs the question... "Why do so many people do this?" and I think there are a number of aspects to the answer of this question:

Self improvement is a really major factor that leads people to change jobs, I think this effect is much stronger than most people give it credit for. A lot of people are ambitious, they want a good career, they want to climb the corporate ladder, be well paid, be important, be respected and the truth is, despite what many of the HR Management text books say, people are not well looked after in most organisations from this viewpoint. There's always a tendency is companies to hire someone, spend some money on training them and then think that they're doing a good job where they are and so they should be left along to do what they're good at. Also, once you've proven that you can do something well, then you'll always have that role, there's very little pressure for change in most companies because why would you fix something that isn't broken. While this may work out fine for all concerned in the short term it doesn't help to employee grow as an individual and sooner or later being placed in a "Pigeon Hole' by their employer will lead to that staff member to look around for the chance to learn new skills and improve their lot in life. This change of role may be to move up the corporate ladder or it may just to be able to undertake a new type of role to provide the chance to learn and practice a new set of job skills. The really unfortunate thing for the firm is that they inevitably lose somebody who knew the organisation well, knew and fit the culture and there is a cost to the organisation for the replacement of such a person.

Other people leave their positions to achieve a degree of self actualization, to test themselves to see what the very best they can ever be is, but starting their own business Under these circumstances there is little that the employer can really do, other than to acknowledge that this will happen from time to time and that effective career planning and succession planning may under some circumstances prevent this.

Others will change jobs to avoid certain managers who have trouble dealing with staff who have made their every day working lives miserable which is a situation that I discuss more in the section of this paperback under Turnover.

Another reason why you might want to change jobs may simply be financial, there may be greener pastures financially in growth industries as opposed to mature industries and growth industries may provide more opportunity for advancement over time. This is something that really belongs to the natural cycle of growth and maturation of companies over time. Those with the ability to reskill and learn quickly are in the position to keep jumping into growth industries as these change over time, being able to identify the growth trends and make the most of the unique opportunities that these growth areas allow.

Pros and Cons

There are distinct Pros and Cons associated with changing jobs at any time:

One of the Cons is the "Better the Devil You Know" syndrome. It's always appealing to think that you can leave what you re doing now and go somewhere to a wonderful new future that better than you're experiencing right now, but is it always going to be like that? Maybe it could be worse, it's always possible? Maybe this rosy image that you have of the future job may not be completely true given the high rate of "fabrication" that I've seen companies put into job descriptions in news papers to attract good staff. There's one thing your current job has going for it, you know what it's all about.

Another Con of moving jobs is that you might not fit the new culture correctly and so may not last there in the long term. This effect can be very strong if you feel a high need for stability and security in yourself. In this case then the prospect of changing jobs can be very scary indeed, but there are also Pros to consider also.

A possible Pro is the ability to use the external job offer as a level to attempt to get more money out of your current employer. On the surface this appears to be intuitively appealing, but in general I've seen that effectiveness of this can vary widely. Even if you do make this work, which may not be easy sometimes then you're in the position where the employer may resent what you did and so when the tables turn at a later date you might not be in such a favourable position. This strategy can be short term gain for long term pain in some cases.

One of the Pros is that often you'll have a better chance of promotion by accepting a job at a higher level than the one that you're currently undertaking. This is by far the easiest way to get a promotion and also by far the easiest way to get a substantial pay rise, since waiting for an internal promotion can be soul destroyingly slow and then even when it does happen the associate may rise may make you wonder why you went to all the effort in the first place. Remember tat the HR and Payroll Departments are there to attempt to reduce your salary to the lowest possible level consistent with you not leaving, but sometimes they miscalculate and you leave, it's only then that they realise they've gone too far and sometimes come back with counter offers. The thing I don't like about counter offers is that it always makes me wonder why they didn't make me the offer in the first place?

Another Pro is the change and the possibility to learn new skills, because no matter how exciting and progressive an employer is, there's a limit to the type and amount of skills you'll have the opportunity to learn and for the newcomers to the job market, the first few years you're working is all about improving your skill set to allow you to climb the corporate ladder and increase your salary. It's well worth making a few moves in the fist five years of your post study employment for this precise reason.

Effects on Climbing the Ladder

The effect on Climbing the Corporate ladder by changing jobs can be very dramatic indeed! Many people have read and heard about the Japanese concept of staying for your entire working career with the one employer but the same definitely does not apply in the western world, in fact, if you've stayed with the one employer for a very long period of time it can be a serious drawback because any new potential employer will feel that you're lacking initiative or that you can't take calculated risks, both of which are highly desirable attributes to have in the current job market, so there is incentive to move around, to change jobs, not only to improve your skill set, learn new thing, but also it's a quicker and easier way to gain promotion and salary rises than staying and being a "faithful" employee in most cases. Of course there's something of a balancing act between changing jobs often to gain new experience and extra status and being seen to be unstable by an employer. A good rule of thumb that a lot of employers use is that two years is considered reasonable to stay at a place of employment. If you have a few stays of less time than this on your resume, then the employer will start to doubt how stable you are and how likely you are to stay with them.

The other thing to consider about changing jobs on your ability to climb the latter is that many firms have their HR policies linked to their Payroll policies, that means, you're locked in where you started so that they don't have to pay you more. So it's very true in a lot of organisations that the point at which you enter the firm is the point at which you're likely to stay and promotion is not likely unless your immediate supervisor leaves and you're the most senior or obviously the best skilled to take the place. If this doesn't happen they you're not likely to get promotion regardless of your efforts or abilities. The only exception to this would be Consulting firms that have some scope to promote within certain ranges because they can have you reporting to a higher level Consultant and promoting you gives them the opportunity to increase you charge out rate to the customer. This is kind of a unique case in that the promotion of staff is linked to the ability of the staff member to bring in revenue for the fir, but it should be note that this is a special case and this case does not hold true in industry.

So for many people changing jobs to work for various employer every couple of years for their first years in the work force is not only a good way to gather valuable experience but it's also the chance to use each shift to gain a promotion each time, since this is a very much easier process than it is to wait for promotion internally, especially in industry and especially in large firms or those with very low staff turnover. In fact the high turnover environment can present great challenges and give an individual great opportunity for growth both in career progression and also salary and for some people it's worth working in a very hard environment with very high staff turnover to get ahead of the pack. The best example I can think of this is mining companies, because they're generally in remote areas they experience high staff turnover, but at the same time they generally pay very well and because the staff turnover is high you can often advance very much quicker in this type of environment than you could in a major city. It's all about lifestyle and your ability to adapt to other lifestyles that you haven't experienced before. If you can live the mining lifestyle in remote areas, then five years there can often give you 10 years worth of experience and career and salary progression and the same applies to overseas postings to the more remote and less exotic and sought after locations.

Your Resume

The resume is the first thing that any prospective employer will see or even know about you, it's the single thing that they will make the decision to interview you, or not interview you from and as a result it should be treated as the very serious document that it really is. Too many people treat their resume as a simple document that they consider some type of formality that's just required to get the interview and as a result, their resumes are not very complete, not very coherent and not very impressive. These people who treat their resumes in such a way tend not to get the very best positions and tend not to get interviews that they really are qualified to attend for the advertised positions.

The typical content for the resume is a summary of your qualifications and experience and really it should be kept as a summary only, with five A4 pages being a good rule of thumb for a maximum. I've resumes covering more than 20 pages it while it's nice to know what a candidate has done, the reality of the situation is that most firms choose to interview far more candidates than they really should and so the person who is conducting the interviews will in practicality will have a very finite time to read and absorb any given resume, so you really need to make maximum impact with that very front page or the interviewer may lose interest in reading the remainder of the document.

The very best thing you can do with your resume is to tailor it in some way to the firm and to the position in question. Surprisingly few people o this and as a result, if you're on of the few that do this, then you'll have an advantage when it comes time for the firm to decide who to call for interviews and who not to call. From my experience it's only a few percent of people that obviously go to this kind of effort and it can be even more effective when it's combined with you doing some research into the firm to try and find reasons why you think you're a match from a skills point of view as well from a culture point of view. If you do this as part of the customisation of your resume you'll probably be in the top one or two percent of those candidates that are being considered providing all you base qualifications are correct and matching what the firm is really looking for.

The other things to really remember about your resume is that it should be accurate and while it's considered fair play to state the magnitude of your past accomplishments to the greatest and most impressive possible extent it's very bad form to actually lie on your resume, which I have seen from time to time, although there are in fact , very few people that really do this, but those that I have seen do this, have done it in such spectacular fashion that it was easy to realise that there were untruthful details in their resume and were easily caught out in the interview process.

Once the resume has been submitted, then you have little choice but to wait for the interview. Calling up to see what's happening regarding your application would only be appropriate after a couple of weeks of no response, because at this stage you have to remember, you've chosen to submit your resume to the firm, they haven't yet reciprocated their interest in you yet. You're in a far stronger position if the firm comes back to you, tan if you go to them at this stage, but there's always that play off to try and decide; calling to ask for progress can be seen as enthusiasm, but it can also be seen as being undesirably pushy. The culture of the firm will generally decide which path is decided upon and at this stage you might not be in a position to know the culture well enough to predict that outcome.

The Interview

This is the key time when you really need to impress the interviewer with your ability not only to "think on your feet", but also perform the task of convincing them interviewer that you're the right person for the position. This means that you have to able to convince them interviewer that your qualifications are right for the position, your experience is right for the position & that you will fit the organisation culturally, because the interviewer is not likely to offer the position unless you're able to providing a level of satisfaction on all three levels. You also have to be able to convince the interviewer that you're able to represent the firm in a competent & professional manner, through dress, language & behaviour.

There's many differing interviewing techniques that firms apply in the work place to try & select the best candidates & some are more effective than others, but one thing to remember when taking interviews is that you'll often have to cross at least two different barriers before gaining a job offer, except in the smallest organisations where the manager hires their own staff directly. In many firms this means that you'll first have to cross the HR manager's interview which will tend to focus on the more general aspects such as the cultural fit rather than qualifications & experience. These will be considered for non technical positions but they will generally only be brushed upon for technical positions. It's important to remember that the HR department understand culture much better than they understand the position descriptions that they often the custodians for, so when dealing with this phase of the process your focus should be to try impress the HR staff with your ability to get along with people & be amiable to work with because these are key things that the HR staff will be looking for when you're talking with them. They'll also be looking for key things such as a degree of enthusiasm, professionalism & motivation to undertake the position.

Once passed this barrier you'll more often be interviewed a second time by the manager who you'll actually be working for when moving onto the job if offered the position. The thing to remember at this interview is that the manager is not an HR person, in fact they may even have some level of contempt for the Hr involvement in the process. This person will not have anything like the same focus as the Hr group, they will be looking very directly at your skill set to determine if you're able to successfully undertake the requirements of the position rather than the more general issues that the HR department focused on. It's important here to ask as may questions as you can about the nature of the work, what is entailed & what is expected of you, this will not only show your interest in the firm & the position but it will also lead to a more thorough understanding of the requirements of the job so that you can decide yourself from a more informed position whether you would accept the position if you're offered it, because while it's nice to be offered positions, it may not always be the best decision to take whatever is offered because it might not be a close fit for you & in the longer term you'll suffer demotivation if you accept the wrong position. Remember the interviewing process is an attempt to match the right person with the right job & while it's true that not all people are right for all positions it's equally true that not all positions are right for all people. I've walked out of interviews that I know that I've done well with, thinking inside myself, "I'll never accept this position if offered it" because I knew it wasn't the right lace for me to be.

When undertaking the interview it's very important that you can make an impression quickly because as I've mentioned before many firms interview far more people that they really need to for most positions & as a result, the interviewer will be undertaking significant workload in addition to their usual duties to do interviews. There won't be time to waste & there won't be a second chance, so you have to impress quickly, not waste time, appear interested but not appear pushy. Appearing pushy can make the manager think that you'll be difficult to deal with in the future & no manager wants to spend time managing difficult staff. It's important to walk that fine line between pushy & enthusiastic.

Some firms use the concept of the "panel" to undertake interviews, where there's several people interviewing at once, asking questions at the same time, the theory being that there will be multiple opinions based on the same information to remove any bias. That's the theory, but I've been through this in practice & I think that the results can be very mixed from such a process. Usually one interviewer dominates the process & so the others become observers & it depends how well the interviewers themselves get along at a work level how consistent the results are. These interviews can be difficult for the interviewee to manage since there will be multiple focus points to manage & often may questions at once. All you can really do in these circumstances it attempt to slow the pace down, answer one question at a time & try spend equal time answering question & asking questions of each of the interviewers, spending perhaps a little more time with the dominant player of the group. Luckily, the "panel" is not often sued & although having two people interview is common, it's often very much less formal than a panel & more closely resembles the traditional one on one interview.

Recruitment Agencies

Recruitment agencies can be a major asset to your career progression in the long term, but they can also be a nuisance if you let them be:

Go recruiters can become valuable aids to help you and your career grow while at the same time the recruiter earns some commissions as you change jobs over the years and the employer gets to hire some top quality staff, it's a win/win/win scenario. I've seen instances where this has happened for mutual benefit and when this happens it's a great result for those involved. This is when the recruiter knows your aspirations, your experience and your abilities, but it takes time to get to that point.

Many recruiters never reach this level and many don't even try to reach this level, trying to earn quick money sending you for interview after interview without much chance of getting the jobs in question, thinking that if they send enough people then sooner or later somebody will secure a job and they'll receive their commission. This is commonly called "The Shotgun Approach", which is generally a waste of time for all concerned. The recruiter themselves waste time lining up a unduly high number of candidates, the candidate spend the time and effort to attend interviews with little chance of actually securing the position and the employer is made to wade through many applicants and undertake many interviews with little success in finding the right person for the right job. The end result of this process is that the recruiter doesn't get a commission because the employer can't find somebody they're happy to place in the job, also the employer is annoyed and upset because of the number of people they've interviewed without success and the candidates are upset because they wasted their tie going for jobs that they weren't likely to get. It's these types of recruiters that are the "Used Car Salesmen" of the recruitment world and unfortunately there too many of them in proportion to the real professionals. These are the type of recruiter that's on the phone to you all the time, getting you to attend interview after interview with no real results, time wasters really.

The important thing to remember is that employers have a job defined, they've typically gone to a lot of work to detail what the job tasks are and what they require in the way of skills from the person who they would offer that job to. Going along unprepared, or going along to a job that you simply don't have close to the required skills for is a waste of tie for all concerned and the employer will view it that way. To get a new job, you have to convince the employer conclusively that you have the correct skill set to match what they're looking for, this is the overriding factor to securing the job, once you've managed to do this the you have to convince them you're a right fit culturally to their firm and then once you've done that then there's the salary negotiation to pass. If you can pas these three hurdles then you should have won the job, but once they start to talk money, you should be quite sure that new position is within your grasp.

Effect on Income

The effect on income of changing jobs can really be quite dramatic at times, especially when you've been in a job for some number of years, because there's always a tendency of companies to award pay rises more or less in line with the inflation figures of the country in which they operate. Outstanding performance may earn a few more percent but don't ever expect pay rises double the inflation figure unless you've just received a promotion, in fact the HR and Payroll policies in most larger companies will ensure that this can never happen, which in itself will add to staff turnover as time progresses.

One of the key features of how much you can improve your financial standing will be how much in demand your skills are at that point in time and also how well the economy is going. If you've got good skills and the economy is booming then you're looking good for a big rise, but remember there is always boom/bust scenarios where people have moved jobs during boom times such as during the .COM boom, later to find that the economy or the industry or both slows down, bankruptcies occur and then they find that they don't have a job after all and so leaving to improve pay may not have been such a good idea in the first place. So the warning is that you can often gain a pay rise and sometimes a very significant pay rise by changing jobs but at the same time there's always the possibility that you can be too greedy and place yourself in a good short term position that in the long term is untenable.

Another factor to consider when changing jobs or thinking about changing jobs is the industry that you're currently working in. Is this industry going places? Will it grow or is it likely to contract? Contracting markets are never good for pay rises, in fact the reverse because as companies go bankrupt and staff are shed and come onto the job market the rates for those in the employment market drop just due to supply and demand factors. If this is a short term effect then it's probably alright to keep looking for work, but sometimes this effect can be along term effect due to market or economic conditions or the simple maturation of the industry and as a result not so many staff are required. Under these circumstances then a change of industry may be your best long term strategy, remembering that if you change industry there's every likely hood you won't as good background and experience in working in that new industry and you may have to take a reduced salary for a couple of years in order to build up the skills required to pursue a higher wage in the future. This type of change can of course be hard to take in the short term, but can be well worth it in the longer term as long as you're carefully selecting the industry and the type of firms that you'll be attempting to enter in the newly chosen industry you're trying to target.

Another good strategy for a medium term advantage is to take a salary drop to enter affirm that may be undertaking some type of project that will enable you to gain valuable job skills that will allow you to enter the contacting market for some time. This is especially the case with the software industry because there are many products that require maybe only one year's experience in order to go contracting with very substantial daily rates. The one primary thing to remember is that if you pursue this option you in effect become tied to the continued success of the software product in question. Continued sales and strength in the product ensures continued success in your ability to contract at premium rates, but a stalling in the sales of the product will result in you looking for new opportunities elsewhere.

Overseas Postings

It was once that if you had an overseas positing on your resume that the world was your oyster, but the effect of the overseas positing on your career prospects is not nearly so clear cut as it was a few years ago. There are many factors to consider now before accepting that overseas position that may seem very lucrative at that point in time when it's offered.

One thing that can have a surprisingly large effect is that of the "Tall Poppy Syndrome". This is stronger in some countries than it is in others & in Australia for example, it's quite strong, not so strong in the USA or the UK. But the effect is that there is a degree of resentment of those who have not done this type of overseas assignment against those who have, also some kind of feelings along the lines of the people staying here working, are just as good as those who have worked overseas. This effect often makes it very hard for those returning from overseas to assume positions back in the own firm that sent them overseas in the first place, since the returning staff will be seen as somebody who perhaps thinks that they're much better than they really are, at least that's the perception. It's very important to start to pan your return home several months before you actually get onto that plane & be sure that the firm is offering you something at least equal to what you gave up before you left. Many people don't do thins to find a very big surprise when they start work back in their own home country. Some find themselves "on the bench", being told that they have to find a position within the firm within a few months or they're redundant & will be treated accordingly, which can be a very big shock for staff who went & worked overseas assuming that they're helping their firm & that the firm will reciprocate one day, often the firm's reciprocation never happens & this is surprisingly common in the real work force, because while you're away overseas, then staff turnover occurs & the people who sent you aren't there anymore, when you return you're just a number & nothing more than that.

Another factor that can have a very big effect on those working overseas is that while you're working in the overseas subsidiary, your base home firms can undertake substantial change & when you return you find that your skills aren't in the same kind of demand that they were in several years before when you were asked or chosen to work overseas. There is always risk of that because often you're being chosen to work overseas because you possess some special skill that the overseas subsidiary requires, but while you're away being a practitioner, then things move on & you being to an extent isolated in a foreign land, are not so able to move along with the progress. It's very important to make sure you're conscious of what's going on back at home & that you stay in contact with your home base & that you insist on the relevant training opportunities. Often though, training alone isn't enough to ensure your relevance in the work place, you may still get the training but not get the job when it's time for you to return.

The best way to counter these detrimental effect sis that when you undertake the overseas posting, do it on the basis that although the firm says they'll have at east an equal position for you when you get back home, don't count on it or expect it. Think in terms of "if there's something there for me when I return, then it's good, but it's not critical & it's not expected", if you approach the overseas position with this in your farmer of mind then you won't be disappointed & you'll be much more thinking about keeping your own skill sets updated as time goes on, irrespective of where you are & what you're doing.

Overseas postings can provide unique career growth opportunities that you could never find back at home, so although there's not always good news with regard to the overseas posting, there can be good news on occasion, where you've gone overseas to gain new skills or perhaps you gone to a country considered out of the way, not one of the tourist locations & the place might be a bit remote. Staff turnover is typically high in such places & so the opportunities for career growth are so much better in places such as these. But always remember, you might or might not go overseas at the request of a company, but once your there & until you return into a position & everything settles down, which doesn't always happen, it's important to remember that you responsibility to your own skills & career growth remain & you need to tend to this the entire time, just as you would have to when you're at home. In this regard the overseas positing is the same as staying at home.

Use of Strategy in Companies

Corporate Strategy

There are many levels of strategy that firms will employ in setting their strategic direction for the future, they are at the Corporate Level, then lower to the Business Unit, Department, Sub Department & then to the individual Managers & Employees, each having their own motivation for things, each having their own priorities for various reasons, some of which for the benefit of the firm, which should always be the case, but sometimes not for the benefit of the firm, but for the benefit of the Strategy maker. In fact, the recent spat of corporate collapses in the USA shows that those setting the strategy at the very highest levels within major firms are not always acting to the benefit of the firm, but that they may be acting to the benefit of themselves.

The whole term "strategy" has been very misused over the past 20 years since it became popular & trendy to use the term & it was often used to describe the naturally longer term timeframes that Asia countries typically use, especially Japan when it comes to dealing with business. In fact, at the time it seemed as though the Asian countries could do no wrong & everyone was clamouring over themselves to become practitioners of Asian Strategy, especially in the West & especially at the highest levels in the firms, but also at the lowers levels with the concepts of Japanese manufacturing being widely employed into the manufacturing firms at the time. Later, as the Communist USSR collapsed, the position of Japan from a military view point was greatly diminished to the Western World, the USA was far less inclined to give Japan the kind of golden deals that they'd enjoyed ever since the end of World War 2, since Japan has always been held up by the west as an example of what cooperation with the west could bring in the way of economic success. At that point recession set in & the Japanese economy started to slow & it's been slow for some time since the, the miracle of Japan was forever shattered as it became more & more Western like in economic terms each day & this process continues despite the Japanese Government's effort to slow the process of change. So Corporate Strategy wasn't synonymous with Japan anymore.

Strategy now for firms has become less of a worshipping of Japan & their economic miracle, but more to some forward thinking about what the firm will be doing in the longer term, although this can be very tricky to attempt to predict. In fact, today firms can be absolutely crucified by the stock market if a single quarter is bad, so there's less & less reason to try thinking long term, the stock market encourages this not to happen but never the less, some attempts at longer term strategic planning would normally be undertaken by most large firms. Considerations for this thought process would be a consideration of whether the markets for the firm's products are expanding or contracting & whether the advent of new products in the near future is likely to alter this situation. This is probably the most critical part of the analysis since a determination of whether the firm is likely to grow or contract is very critical to you as an employee of the firm. If the prediction is for growth, then that means opportunities both in the way of salary growth but also career growth & opportunities for advancement, but if that prediction is for contraction, that often means no growth opportunities, salary or career growth. Inn fact, I have many colleagues that upon hearing the prediction for contraction as a result of Strategic Planning Session instantly contact their usually recruitment agencies using the theory that it's not even worth waiting to see the outcomes because it will be painful to stay with that firm. Some go further than this, not relying on the management of the firm to make the decisions due to mistrust of their ability to make a true prediction of the future due to self interest, they make their own decisions about the future of the firm & act upon the results accordingly themselves. Regardless of who is doing the Strategic Planning for the firm, those outcomes from the process have a very direct & powerful effect on your own career prospects for the future. I myself think that it is often a waste of time staying with a firm that predicts a bleak future. If you're going to spend a lot of your time at work, working for somebody else it may as well be as pleasant as possible & struggling with lack of career growth & lack of salary growth can be very demotivating over the longer term, it's better to look for those greener pastures elsewhere, because even if the economy is suffering, there will usually be greener pastures somewhere.

Departmental Strategy

Once the high level strategy of the firm has been determined & the plan set forth from the highest levels of the firm, then Business Units or Departments will construct their own strategies in an attempt ascertain how each group of the firm will attempt to contribute to the common good, consistent with the overall strategy. There are definite dimensions to this level of strategy, that of the department, business unit or group in itself & those of the manager who is running the group. I will describe the Boss' Strategy & how it interacts with the Corporate Strategy in the net Section in this book. This next section will focus much more on what happens in the real world while this section will refer to what ought to be happening in the more ideal circumstances.

Once the firm has decided what the longer term strategies are to be, it's up to each of the Business Units, Departments or Groups to devise their own strategies to support the overall high level strategies of the firm. There are a number of layers to this strategy & its support, but typically strategy issues are concerned with issues such as the following at the higher level & those strategies at the Departmental level are generally in support of these factors:

1. Will the firm grow or contract
2. Are the product offering of the firm likely to alter this view
3. Are the competitors likely to increase or decrease risk to the firm, what will they be doing over the same time frame & what should the firm be doing to counter the actions of the competitors
4. Will the economy be conducive to growth or contraction
5. How will good staff be retained, especially in contraction conditions
6. Is new technology likely to change the current situation in any way
7. Is the Government likely to change things in any way
8. Are major infrastructure purchases likely

All of the factors listed above can have a very major impact upon the ability you'll have to grow in your career, the opportunities & the ability that you'll have for your salary to grow over time as you stay with the firm. Item 1) is probably the single largest determinate of you career growth at the firm, quite irrespective of you actual performance, because if the firm is contracting then no matter how well you perform, you'll be very limited in terms of growth opportunities & salary increments. It's almost to the point that if you're working for a firm that is substantially contracting or even predicting it to the point where it's forming part of the strategy of the firm, they you're probably better off leaving. Items 3) & 4) have very similar effects, but if the entire economy is contracting & it's not just the firm or the industry where you're working, then leaving is not such a good thing to do. Under these conditions it's usually better to stay put & hide from the bad economy for some time until the bad times pass by.

Items 2) & 8) are unusual in that even in a contracting firm, the ability for you be become involved in a new product that is predicted or even hoped to turn around the bad fortunes of the firm can provide helpful career opportunities. Mind you, there will be very limited ability under these circumstances for you to gain in the way of financial rewards but you'll at least be able to gain valuable experience in such an environment that you can later sell to other firms in the way of a higher salary. Items 6) & 7) are also similar in effect to this also, but if the government is intervening to protect your firm or your industry, that's usually a sign of things not being sustainable over the longer term & it's also time to leave the firm & possible the industry also.

Item 5) is usually the one that most firms forget or implement very poorly. Bad times are something that sets off alarm bells with workers, silent ones, inaudible to managers, but they're there never the less. The staff starts to think about the future & about their role with the firm & maybe even the survivability for the firm in the longer term. This in itself can be the root cause of massive staff losses & the first staff to leave are those with portable skills that can be moved to other firms easily in demand areas. Given that it's often reported that a single staff turnover can cost as much as 100% of an annual salary to recover, it's surprising that this is often ignored, but then again, it comes back to management viewing the current situation & dealing with the current situation rather that what might happen in the future due to the incentives of their reward structure which are typically short termed.

The Boss' Strategy

Once the high level strategy of the firm has been determined & the plan set forth from the highest levels of the firm, then Business Units or Departments will construct their own strategies in an attempt ascertain how each group of the firm will attempt to contribute to the common good, consistent with the overall strategy. At least, it would be really nice to think that this is what really happens in the real world, but the truth is that once you start to drop levels below the very highest management of the firm, the amount of office politics & self interest increases very dramatically. This is because often it's group manager themselves that constructs their own strategy with little hindrance from the highest level manager because they feel their job is done. With the very high level of autonomy that managers typically have with the setting of their own strategies, the self interest factor is very greatly increased in the equation & often it's a matter of what isn't said in the manger's setting of strategy that's more important for the individual than what is said.

Many managers will in their own mind turn setting the strategy of their department into a setting of strategy for their own personal career paths at the expense of everything else in their departments. Many managers are able to rationalize this in their own minds thinking that it's their own department, there fore all the resources that are available to that group are therefore theirs to use at their own discretion, others think more in terms of, they've worked hard for years & so it's only their just reward that they have all these resources available to them to allow their careers to grow even more. Either way, many managers feel it's their right to use the resources of the firm for their very own benefits. Sometimes this can be bad for the employee but sometimes this can be good if you're well aligned with your employer with regard to the future. If you're not well aligned with what your manager is doing & planning for the future then this situation will not be a good situation for your future with the firm. Being well aligned with your managers means something like; you're going to spend some time with the firm, some time with the manager that you're currently working for & that you'll be attempting to expand your skill base in a field that is totally consistent with the department or group that you're currently working for & what is planned for the group by your manager. If however, you're looking for a career change in direction & you're planning not to stay with the firm for too long, or panning not to stay with your current manager for too long or you're obviously not gaining experience directly relevant to your current department or group then you'll have definite clash of interests with your manager. Some managers are very much more mature than other when it comes to the realisation that some staff member are making the firm & the department that they're currently working in, a "stepping stone" towards bigger & better things elsewhere in the future. I've personally had trouble in this area myself, where a manager of a rival department to the one I was currently working for offered me a position with his group, he was one of those "Stars" that I spoke of earlier with a mandate for change in his field, but the problem for me was that I was using the firm that I was currently working for as a "Stepping stone" to get away from Engineering & was looking for a shift into IT. The manger at hand just didn't understand this at all, since he was totally internally focused on his own Engineering career & couldn't even consider that somebody would want to leave the profession. As a result there was bad blood between us when I didn't accept his position & things were only reconciled between us after I accepted an IT position & personally helped out his department on a number of occasions. I'd proved to him, that my desire to move had in fact been the right thing for me to do for me, even though it wasn't necessarily the best thing for him, but it was only after I could show proficiency & help him & his own ambitions that he could accept the outcome & my own agenda.

The Strategy of the Individual

At the individual level, strategy really means the personal aspirations of the individual with regard to their intended future direction in their career path. When considering this with regard to the individual there are usually very distinct short & long term aims that most employees will be considering which may be in very direct contrast with each other at times. For example, the short term aspiration for the staff member may be to do some training over the next few months that will lead to a pay rise later in the year. In the longer term the employee may be saving up enough money to move to another city & pursue their own business in a totally different industry, one that at present is in their lives in the way of a hobby or pastime, so the short term & the long term can really be very different from one individual to another.

Short term career strategies are very much more likely to revolve around the firm that the individual is currently working for & the industry in which they're currently working. Short term objectives for the individual employee will typically be things like:

1. Training
2. A Project at Work
3. Trying to Position for Promotion

While the longer term strategies for the individual tend to me more lifestyle choices that work may be a part of:

1. Retire at a Certain Age
2. Undertake a Degree Study to change career industries
3. Move to another country
4. Start their own business

Often the two are in very direct conflict & this can be very difficult to manage when it becomes known to your manager that your longer term ambitions don't lie with the current firm. Some manager take the philosophical approach, thinking that such things are part of the cycle of nature, people come & go, but the creature, the firm keeps on going & nobody is indispensable. Some managers are much more childish about it & they feel that longer term ambitions that are not totally consistent with the firm that the employee is working for is a type of treason that should be punished & I have heard stories of staff being fired from jobs because they made their longer term ambitions known to the wrong person, although I have not personally witnessed this.

One thing to remember, don't let you personal long term ambitions become too public unless you really are planning to stay with the firm or unless you know your manager will react in a favourable manner to this. If long term ambitions away from the firm are well known, then this can put you into a bad position with regard to your ability to grow in your career, since many managers will feel if there's a choice to make for promotion or personal growth opportunities, it's better to give it to the person they believe will be staying with the firm in the long term. Consequentially, you could easily miss out on the best opportunities for career growth & this in itself may inhibit your ability to realise you long term goals. Even if you do feel your manager is not going to react badly to long term aims out of the firm, remember that manager's come & go just like staff, once it's known that your ambitions lie outside the firm it can become self fulfilling as managers change & the new manager may take resentment to your aims, even though your manager at the time was fine with the idea.

Strategy Interactions

From the above discussion, it can be seen that at differing levels within the firm at any point in time there's many conflicting & differing strategies operating at once. With the many direct conflicts that are usually coincident, it's not surprising that many firms cannot effectively implement changes in strategies when they keep largely the same staff at all levels & the same type of operations, there's just too many vested interests in the outcomes & too many personal agendas being operated for it to all work together. I've seen many firms that have hit upon bad times & they're realised this is occurring early in the piece & have correctly attempted to formulate strategies to arrest the decline. The strategies have been quite reasonable & logical but the implementation has failed badly & the efforts seen by the staff to change things have been felt to have been very poor & why is this? Because the highest level of management have naively felt that if the decide on a new strategy & they tell the next level of managers down the hierarchy what this is then it will all happen & everything will be sorted out & in a short time the firm will be back on it's feet, while in reality, nothing could be further from the truth.

Typically the highest level of management is so separated from the operation levels of the firm, especially in large firms that they cannot effectively communicate with the operational layer. They have to communicate to the next level down of the middle level managers who can then get directly to the operations, but the difficulty is that the middle level rarely has incentive to change because they're working in systems with established powers bases that everyone is comfortable working with, nobody at the middle level wants this to change as each is happy that they have the resources of their own department available to them to enhance their own longer term career potential. Attempts by the highest level manager to communicate with the operational level of the firm are typically ignored by the lowest level because they feel that their order are taken from their immediate supervisors, especially since it's this person who decides their pay rises each year. Attempts by the highest level manager to communicate with the operational levels of the firm via the middle level managers will also fail, but they will fail due to the deliberate non-communication of new directions by the middle level managers & also because the middle level managers are not likely to implement support structures consistent with the achieving of the strategies that the highest level of management are striving for.

I have worked for firms that have had so much trouble with this type of communication issue & their lack of success implementing new strategies that the firm nearly went bankrupt because there were department sales & purchases which resulting in essential parts of the business for some of the remaining units being sliced off & very dysfunctional pieces left behind. The management of the firm tried everything to try & prevent this from occurring but the vested interests of the firm prevented wide scale changes from occurring, but things kept getting worse & worse. In the end the firm cut staff very severely to remove the past & moved buildings to remove the past also. In fact, many managers feel that the very best way to achieve change is to move building into a place physically smaller than was previously the case to create the impression that staff have to go. Under these circumstances staff will generally be more receptive to the direction of their superiors, at least, that the theory anyway. So it can be concluded that the implementation of new strategies by the highest levels of the firm can be very difficult in practice and often the interaction of the differing point of view & strategies of the differing levels of the firm will often be at odds with each other preventing progress with regard to new directions in strategy.

Group Think

Group Dynamics in the Office

Group Dynamics in the office can have a profound effect on the working conditions that you'll experience in the firm. Some firms encourage growth & original thinking, but this in the real world is not so common. More common is the whole culture of "Group Think", which has been defined as:

"A mode of thinking that people engage in where they are deeply involved in a cohesive in-group, where the members' striving for unanimity overrides their motivations to realistically appraise alternative courses of action."[2]

Group think of this type is very common in the office to the point in some firms where they simply cannot make sensible decisions because there are one or two dominant people in the firm with their very own set views which may or may not represent the firm as a whole. With these people forcefully giving their view & the other blindly accepting what is put forward then the best outcomes for the firm may not always be possible. In this type of culture, it's not the decision that's important but the cohesion of the group, the ability for the group to think & passively act together as if the outcome in itself is of no importance. This is especially the case in the Public Sector where people who speak forcefully seem to be accepted as being subject matter experts in their field, whether this be true or not. There's a kind of thinking along the lines, that if somebody speaks forcefully enough about an issue then they must really know that issue very well, but in the public Sector this is often just a bluff tactic & the real subject matter experts are sitting quietly in the corner working away. In fact, the art of talking over the top of others is very well developed in the Public Sector because it's very much the loudest voice wins the argument, logic & reason often not being major factors in the making of decisions.

Other firms, can go to the other extreme & use the concept of individual accountability to the point where it doesn't make sense, but the concept is so ingrained in the firm that they can't see away from this. While firms of this type are generally fewer in number than those accepting the group as the norm, they do exist & these types of environments lead themselves open to the use of the "Cannon Fodder" tactic that managers often use in such environments.

Some firms adopt the strategy that the Japanese use of making decisions in large groups, the logic being that everybody in the group becomes a stake holder in the decision & therefore has an interest in the outcome. While this may work well in Japan, it loses something when it's converted to the Western world because it fails to consider that there's elements in the workforce in the western world that don't really care what the outcome is, which is a very unfortunate thing to say, but the reality is that this is true in many Blue Collar environments. This attitude is brought about the by unionization of some industries where the firm & the management of the firm are thought of as enemies & the worker has difficulty seeing the direct relationship between their own performance at work & the performance of the firm in the long term & therefore their own job security. In such environments the group decision making process will gravitate towards a very few people actually participating the in decision process & the majority sitting back with blank minds with little input to the process. In fact many will totally avoid saying anything at all either through simply not caring what the outcome will be or through their need to conform to the group as a whole & not wanting to be seen to be out of place with the group & their work colleagues. In these circumstances the whole concept of group decision making almost disappears because although there are numbers present, there's very little new & creative thought being undertaken & those that re present are certainly not taking ownership of the process or the outcomes.

The whole "Group Think" concept can become the silent force that shapes many decisions or many indecisions as the case may be in some firms. The culture of the firm may simply not allow group based decision making to undertaken in any kind of sensible manner.

Social Norms and Expected Behaviour

Social norms & expected behaviour can vary very dramatically from one organization to the next & much of this is governed by the way that groups react & work together in the firm. As said before people strive for anonymity because it gives them a feeling of a lack of accountability in the outcomes decided upon & many also feel that group decision making is something that in effect relieves any one single person of being individually accountability.

This issue of individual accountability is really a very serious one in many firms & especially in the Public Sector in as much as people are happy generally to provide their best efforts & their best care when undertaking work, but not many actually willing to make themselves personally accountable for the outcomes, but in many firm/customer situations, the customer is actually paying for a service & so it makes sense that somebody from the supplying firm should be accountable for the delivery & customer satisfaction of the service. In general you'll find that the salaries paid for that accountability are very much higher than for the nameless faces that don't accept that responsibility. There are other firms however, that are so fixated with the process of group decision making because they are trying to emulate the Japanese successes of 10 years ago, they refuse to pay the decision makers more than the followers & of course this leads to the situation where those decision makers will start to feel demotivated over time since they're the risk takers, the ones that will lead the firm to success & they're also thee ones putting their necks on the line for no substantial rewards. In these types of organizations the actually process has become more important than the actually result & there are many firms that have lost their way to this extent because the HR Departments are there in the background insisting upon stringent adherence to the rules of the decision making process & completely losing sight of the fact that in the Western World very much more than in Japan, there are leaders & there are followers. The difference between the workers & the staff are very much higher in the West than they are in Japan

& thinking that Japanese Group Dynamics will automatically translate to the West is just completely erroneous. For the newcomer to the workforce, this type of situation provides the unique opportunity for staff to become part of the decision making process & the opportunity to become involved at levels in which they would normally have to wait years for. This is invaluable experience, but given the Group Structure in place it might not be so easy for you to represent this in your resume, since any attempt by a prospective employer could lead to the situation where they're told by previous employers that you were merely one of a team.

In other firms where the Group Decision making process works, are much more likely to have a very close relationship between the management & their staff. Under these circumstances the management of the firm are much more able to work as "Coaches" for the newer & less experienced staff. But the one thing remains is that there are many ways that the firm will deal with the issues of expected behaviour & social norms, but one thing to remember, if you want a nice quite comfortable life, then don't do or say too much different from the group, but if want to use the situation to your advantage then you have the opportunity to become involved in decisions & the implementation of those decisions

Stomp on Anyone Different (Anyone Different = Troublemaker)

In most firms, being too different is nothing less than a cardinal sin that can never be redeemed under any circumstances. Different has a number of aspects to it, for some being different means that you arrive at work at a different time to most of the other, for some it means having a different preference for rewards for good work, it could be the preference for working from home where it's available or wanting career advancement way beyond their peers or whatever. The real issue for most firms for those that are different is that their reaction under the influence of pressure or difficult time is not known like it is for the bulk of the work force & these people are seen as potentially destabilizing by the manager they work for. In fact, some manager are so worried by having staff that they see as being different that they'll actively pursue a policy of ridding themselves of such staff if they can. Another fear that managers may have about these kinds of staff is that anyone who stands out as different may be somebody capable of their own thought processes which is not desirable in most structured environments & so the excuse that that person doesn't fit the "culture" of the organisation is often sued as an excuse to have them removed from their position.

The drive for anonymity in some firms is so strong that it actually drives some people to be different, they feel that conforming to the group as much as they see in front of their eyes at the office is enough to drive them to distraction & so they cry out in an attempt to gain an degree of individuality, but this can often be the start of their problems with their working environment rather than the conclusion of the problem. Once people appear to be too different to the group norms that have been establish by the firm then people start to wonder about the culture of the firm & whether this person really fits in or not & people who are seen not to fit in are seen as not team players & as such not given the same opportunities as the others who follow in quiet, never criticizing & also never contributing to the outcomes that the firm is driving for.

Many manager will feel that staff that act too differently are difficult to manage since it makes sense for a manager that everyone behave much the same so that the management can set in place decisions & structures that suit the established norms of the firm. People who lay outside the norms require special effort & because of that, they're not really desirable. This attitude can extend into all kinds of areas, from the actually front line of the working place as far as into the HR Department. The best example I can think of this is that many USA based firms provide medical insurance as part of their salary packages, but in some countries there's Government based health schemes rendering the private schemes provided by the employer redundant to some extent. Many of the younger workers of the firm would prefer not to have a large portion of their salary packages paid in medical insurance since they're not likely to use it & they see it as a waste which for many younger works it is, but the HR department will typically cling to rigid rules that require the staff to take substantial portions of their salary in this way. The norms of the firm have established how people should take their salary packages & anyone who critics this approach will be called a trouble maker because they're not conforming to the norms of the firm, even though these norms may not suit a sub section of the staff of the firm.

Many firms have an unofficial policy of trying to weed out anyone different to the average, be they very good performer or very bad. The bad performs are typically told they're redundant when a "down sizing" occurs, which the very good performer are weeded out through more subtle methods such as lack of career growth opportunities or lack of reasonable salary increments, but the effect is much the same in the long term.

Technology "Helping" Business

The PC

Probably nothing in the office environment in the past 100 years has had the impact upon how business is done & what work is done in the office that the PC. The first PC's were 1Mhz monsters that had very modest amounts of memory & even more modest operating systems that required you to learn command lines & you really had to know what you were doing to drive them. I can myself remember learning operating systems commands so that I could drive the first PC's that I had to work with & while it seemed a bit of a trial at the time I become proficient to the point where it took me a long time to switch to the newer more graphical based operating systems because there simply wasn't any productivity increase for me in making the change. In fact, the first time I saw graphical based operating systems I thought it was a waste of tie because it didn't give you anything else that you didn't already have & that was true of the earliest version of the graphical operating systems. But today PC's are everywhere in every office & if you don't know PC technology, then your career possibilities in an office environment are very limited indeed. The time frame over which this has occurred is approximately 15-20 years which isn't really a long time in the cycle of a workers lifetime & this only goes to amplify the point made earlier that you have to keep your skill set up to date & it's nobody else's business but you own to ensure that you do that. Failure to do so can render you unemployable for all intensive purposes, so it's critical to keep up to date at all times. This is sometimes easier for men to do rather than women because traditionally women have left the workforce for some time to have & raise the family while the man continues to work & during this time technology passes by & when the woman wants to reenter the workforce there's technology gaps that she has to catch up & so retaining her original position can be difficult I think.

PC's have managed to get their ways into everything in the past 20 years, from being almost a curiosity, into every office, process based systems, scientific systems, even down to simple functions like balancing the family budgets & of course the big business of games. Which leads to the issue of software used in business, I think almost every single PC in use in any business that I have ever been to work with has had illegal software on it, despite the best efforts of the firm to eradicate it & some firms do go to great lengths to try & eradicate it or this is my gut feel anyway, although often it's difficult to really know for sure. The reason why it's difficult to really know is that many firms have standard PC "builds" that are supplied to the field & so it's not really well known out on the field at the operation al level exactly what is supposed to be on the PC & because it's known well known what is supposed to be there, then it's obvious based on that, that it's also hard to know what shouldn't be there. With this there's the obvious loss of productivity that comes with the use of illegal software since most illegal software in use in offices today has little to do with the actual work being undertaken, although illegal software being used to enhance productivity of staff would represent about 20% & this is mostly done in very large firms where the process of getting software authorized for use by a few individuals is so difficult that the firm almost forces their staff to use unauthorized software to get their jobs done. Although some illegally used software is productivity based it's true to say I think that the large majority has nothing to do with the work being done at the firm & includes such things as chat software, something to do with personal hobbies or game & with the use of this software there's the obvious loss of the time of the staff being diverted onto non productive tasks. So while it's true to say that in many ways the PC has rough with it productivity gains in the way of Word Processors, Spreadsheets, project Management Software, Process Systems, it's also brought with it the ability for staff to waste a lot of time & look productive at the same time.

The other major thing that the PC has managed to do is to drive power away from those old fashioned IT departments in firms where the IT department held a lot of power in central databases & made it very difficult for this to find it's way to the actually users & owners of that data. In fact many firms has It departments in the past that were totally lacking in any kind of customer focus & they were operating almost at the extent where you'd be expected to wear a white coat to walk into the department. Luckily the PC gave power back to the users & owners of the data but what it did at the same time was give a huge amount of power to those who weren't necessarily ready for it. Islands of automation sprang up all over the firm as did disparate databases & the firm moved from one central database under the pure data view of the world in the central IT department to having data everywhere, so much so that nobody could actually identify where it was & often it was assumed to have not been collected when in reality several groups had collected the same data over time, put it into different places & had simultaneously spend money on it's maintenance. So while to some extent it's very true to say that the PC put power into the hands of the users it has in some firms put chaos into the storing of & especially the retrieval of corporate data.

The Network

The network would have to go down as the most unreliable weak link in most office IT infrastructure, but it has improved markedly in the past five years or so. When the network was first created, it was a way of one or more PC's to share data. They were in the first instance, incredibly unreliable & the network operating systems were generally poorly understood by their support staff who often struggled to keep them running. Later as the network started to get more reliable then the firm would put application software onto network servers which meant that the distribution & maintenance of PC's was reduced. While this was fine as long as everything was working fine, the fact that the software was on the server meant that unreliable servers or networks meant unreliable availability of services to the staff to use. Often, even now in some firms we can see worker sitting around with literally nothing to do because their network isn't available or it's too slow to actually use.

The other great idea that the network could help with is backup, it was often circulated that if you put your vital data onto a network drive it would be backed up, but I've seen no end of problems at firms trying to recover backups & often this simply can't be done, making the whole backup argument hollow in some firms. Form my own personal experience I'd be much more happy & go to bed with a more secure feeling at night if I backed up my hard drive onto an external hard disk backup unit than to the network, because in my experience if the PC does crash there's about 20% chance I'll actually get my data back from the network backup.

The other hot issue about networks is security because these systems contain a lot of corporate data, security is an important issue. Many firms go to great lengths to attempt o define the security rules that will be applied across the organization & sometimes to no avail. A form that I worked with applied a very stringent set of rules to the staff as the their password rules. The password has to be eight or more characters long, it had to contain at least one number & had t have a mix of upper & lower case & could not contain any work used in the English dictionary & it also remembered the 100 passwords that you'd used before to prevent you using passwords too often. This sounds very secure – right? The problems was that it was so secure that nobody could use the systems because they couldn't log in. Many of the staff at this site were tradesmen, men who were employed because of their skills in metal welding, boiler making, machining & such like & they were using the systems at the firm to keep track of Plant Maintenance & when the new rules were imposed, without nay prior warning of course most of the staff couldn't successfully pick a new password & so were locked out & those that did manager to accidentally guess something that qualified under the new rules gave their user identification & their passwords to all their work buddies so that they could keep working. The sit went from a reasonable degree of security to having none at all because huge number of staff were using just a few passwords & many could not retrieve the data that they needed to perform their daily tasks.

So the network is a very much maligned piece of infrastructure in most firms & deservedly so in some cases. The issues of access, reliability & bandwidth continues to plague most firms & many firms have trouble grappling with these issues every day. Working with networks will no doubt provide good career paths in the future, probably even more so than they do now, much in the same way that the Database Administrator became a highly sought after position in the past 10years, the Network Administrator &

Architect will continue to see a rise in their status over time over the next 10 years as many firms realise the potential of this piece of infrastructure, but at the same time realise the current issues with it need to be addressed by the best available staff in many firms.

The Mainframe

Many firms actually have a lot of unresolved issues with the Mainframe & the use of it. Such fundamental issues such as who owns the data is not resolved satisfactorily at a lot of firms & many firms have a lot of people squabbling over this very issue. In many firms the IT department is the custodian of the Mainframe & everything on it because many firms view the information on this machine as critical & also potentially sensitive & there's no doubt that there is sensitive information on most Mainframes such as payroll information that many firms wish to apply stringent security to. This is the only one thing that the mainframe truly does in a much better manner than any of the smaller servers that are being used in most firms, it's the issue of security. A good general rules to apply is that the bigger the machine, the better the security is on it. Many firms with critical information will find this absolutely necessary to their operations, while for other it's not such an issue, more its rather a case of ensuring that nobody accidentally does anything stupid & deletes anything important. BBut for the very large firm the security provisions of the Mainframe really is worth the expenditure, even if it's not worth it in a any other area. The downside with the Mainframe is security also! Because once things are on the Mainframe, they're really hard to get back out in a useful manner for the staff on site at the operational level to sue their information in any meaningful & profitable way. The IT department can write reports, but it's true to say that most IT departments really don't see this as their prime focus in life. In fact, quite the reverse, because most It Manger's for the sake of their own careers like to focus on the development of new software by large teams of people. After all, there's no glory in putting on your resume that you manager five people mostly maintaining bought systems when you could say that you managed a Project team of 20 people who were designing & developing new systems, the latter is so much better on a resume for an IT Manager & so much better for that IT Manager in terms of the dollars that they're likely to be able to ask for & receive when applying for new jobs. So while it's true to say that the security feature are the very best features of the mainframe it's also true to say that it's these very features that make the retrieval & use of the data very difficult in practice.

The other issue about the Mainframe is the cost, sometimes the cost of purchasing parts, expansion capacity & running costs can be totally ridiculous. I know of one example where a firm was under contract with their outsourcer for the use of mainframe machines. They quietly paid their money each year, never questioning the amount because this firm was government owned. They decided that they needed to buy some new systems to perform Plant Maintenance & at the same time they got a quote for facilities management. The software firm gave two prices, one for a Mainframe based systems which was originally asked for & also an alternate with a mini computer server as the database & application software server. The difference was huge they questioned the quote & after this being reaffirmed took the second option, much to the displeasure of their IT department. They went & bought the second largest mini computer server that this manufacturer made, which was so big that they'd never sold one before in that country! & they did that merely because it as so much cheaper than what they were used to paying & it would provide five years expected growth. The whole project was completed on time & on budget, return on investment in five months & reports that used to take virtually the whole day to run we re running in seconds. In fact I was called to look a report that "wasn't running" only to find that it was functioning completely correctly but it was running so fast that the users thought it couldn't possibly be working correctly.

Of course this was a special case where the firm had been broken into a number of pieces & the pieces were much smaller than the original. One thing that the Mainframe does well is to scale to the very largest firms. There is a point at which you become so large that you have no choice but to use a Mainframe, but in the case above the firm was one of these largest firms that had no choice, but as being broken into smaller discrete firms, each of which was now small enough to make their own choices.

Corporate Data

One of the biggest hot issues in the IT arena is that of corporate data, what is it & who owns it? It's never easy to quantify the answers to these questions & many firms have spend millions of dollars attempting to answer this & also attempting to answer who should model such data & is this modeling of a corporate data model any use even if it were to be done.

As for the issue of corporate data many firms really struggle every day with the issues of who owns that data that is collected, at least there's no arguments over who collects the data since this is often very obvious. But the issue of who owns the data is one of the hot potatoes that many firms cannot resolve since the ownership of the data implies the ability to use that data & the have the funding to maintain & use the tools that allow the access to that data & when it comes to budget time then everyone is interested because budgets are hard to get in most firms. In a lot of firms the fact that the corporate data is typically stored on a Mainframe computer that the IT department owns give the IT department the advantage in the struggle for power. They quite effectively argue that because the data is stored on their machine they must own that data & even though this argument makes no sense at all, many higher level manager fall for the argument & let the IT department be the owners & users of the data for their own devices. Once this occurs that data that the user community so diligently collects generally disappears from visibility & they have no access to that data to use for the daily operations of the firm. Typically the IT will write a few standard reports because they feel that they should & after that the whole issue of data analysis for the business is a dead issue as far as the It department is concerned. They're simply not interested.

Many IT departments simply make no attempt to provide that much needed thing that the users of the data cry out for every day, data analysis tools & staff. Many firms struggle with this & in many firms there the issue that IT logically would own such a person because they would need access to corporate data, but if they had the budget o provide such a person, they'd rather spend the money elsewhere. If the users had the funds for such a position then the IT department would see this as an encroachment on their area of operation & would attempt to resist the individual by restricting their access to the tools necessary to do the job. It's with these contrary positions that the users & collectors of the data continue to argue with the custodians of the data.

The other hot issue is that of the modeling of the data for corporate use. Many firms have been conned into thinking that this is worthwhile exercise by the database vendor. Some of their It staff attend courses in data modeling & come out convinced that the data model of the firm is the be all & end all of all the problems that the IT department will ever have. Of course database firms have a very vested interest in this type of exercise because for them, the use of their tools in the modeling of the firm & the construction of systems to hang off the model makes it difficult for pre built software to be purchased & installed without major disruption to this process. In fact, if this policy is pursued with enough vigor then it becomes almost impossible for the firm to purchase packed enterprise software because it will typically be something more akin to an industry "best practices" (best practice is talked about later in this book), rather than trying to model all the nuisances & bad practices that the firm has employed over the previous years. Thankfully, the number of firms that have decided to embark on this typically futile & pointless exercise is dropping, since managers are starting to realise that in such turbulent times such as now, things simply don't stand still & that any attempt to model the entire firm from a data perspective from the point of view of data is doomed to failure because of the changes that most firms are experiencing every day. Once the model is finished then it's immediately out of date & probably will never be sued or relevant because of this. Many firms have spent a lot of money on this exercise only to find out later that the money was wasted.

Software Acronyms

Acronyms are a major source of distraction to the end users when the It staff start to use them. It's almost as if they've invented their own language in order to confuse others & I'm reminded of the Tarot cards that were changed from one way up with one meaning to both ways up in order to make it more complicated for people to read them, I think the IT industry is guilty of the same thinking in a lot of ways, but having said this the IT industry is at least very deregulated in how it operates & doesn't have much in the way of self protection that's employed by other profession with Doctors, Lawyers & Accountants springing to mind, each having very specific monopolies bestowed upon them by the governments around the world. In fact, the IT industry in a lot of countries actually has the government working against the individuals that it employs with many governments having special immigration rules for IT professionals that make it much easier for people with IT skills to move from the non developed world to the developed world with nursing being the only other profession that springs to mind that often subjected to the same effect. It could be argued that this lowers the salary levels of the local staff, but at the same time the employers would argue that the shortages of local staff require them to pay higher wages. Of course the governments have to attempt to play the balancing act between the two conflicting interests. So for the It professional, although the acronyms are thrown around often with no good reason other than in an attempt to sound to be educated to their peers this is a rather mild & even if annoying for of segregation from other professions compared with what goes on in some other industries.

Consultants "Helping" Business

The "Cow From Out of Town" Story

I was once told the "Cow From Out of Town Story" by an Indian friend of mine. He was a colleague that often shared his "Pearls of Wisdoms" with us non Indians & although much of what he said was greeted with roars of laughter because his was something of a comedian & his timing was often perfect, his meaning underneath was often exactly correct & this story was one of those hidden truths.

The story went along the lines of that people will pay more for a cow from another village than from their own. The logic & reason being that if it's from another village then it must be one of their best ones, they wouldn't want to lose face by sending a bad one & so it must be good. Also if it's from another village then it must have learned some really good tricks that the local cows wouldn't have been exposed to. Because of this it must be a good one & we had better be prepared to pay more than we would for a local one.

Although this might sound like backward misguided logic, it often holds true in the corporate world, especially when it comes to the staff that companies employ. I've seen it so often that firms won't listen to their own staff when problems are reported or solutions are given & then the firm will pay a lot of money for an external consultant to be brought in to work on the same problem & everyone is very happy with the result when the consultant comes to the same conclusion as the staff had done so themselves. I always wonder why it is that somebody from outside the firm has to tell a manager something before they'll take notice.

Some of this I'm sure has to do with selecting scape goats, since some managers are looking for an external person to blame if things go wrong after the recommendations are implemented & this is very often the case in the Public Sector where managers will bring in consultant after consultant until their preferred recommendations are given as advise. I myself have been on such assignment where the staff of the firm have said; "Oh, you're here to look at that? It's very strange you're about the fifth person to have looked at that issue in the past year or so". Once you hear that you know the manager is weak willed & attempting to pre organize a scape goats in case anything goes wrong.

Another factor in this is that many managers simply don't trust the abilities of the staff to do anything other than the normal routine, mundane activities. Many managers have a very poor image of their staff & this is amplified if they didn't select the staff themselves but inherited staff after being promoted or being hired into a position where the staff had already been incumbent which is almost always the case except for start up firms. Many hold the vie that they're inherited a bunch of dunces & that had they been allowed to select their very own staff things would be much better, so even if the staff are capable many managers are dismissive of the new ideas of their staff & some managers are thinking of using some of their staff as Cannon Fodder at a later date if the need ever arises.

But no doubt there is a factor that can be attributed to the "Cow From Out of Town" concept as many manager feel that somebody from outside the organisation will have learned some good tricks like the cow from the other village would have done, despite the fact that there can be absolutely no evidence that that effect. So although many firms will hide & explain the use of outsiders for some types of work on the basis that external skills that don't exist within the firm are required to do the job, it's much more often on the basis that they don't trust their staff with any real intelligence or they really want to be prepared to have a scape goat if the need arises to protect their own lack of decision making ability.

Types of Consultants

Many people out there in industry tar "Consultants" with the same brush but in reality there are a myriad of types of Consultants, each with their very own unique value proposition which can very markedly from firm to firm & from Consultant to Consultant. There's something of a continuum going from the hard edge technical Consultant who is typically brought in for a set period of time or to perform a set series of tasks to the other end of the spectrum being something like HR or Management Consultants whose deliverables can be rather vague at time.

It should also be noted that in general full time employees do not like consultants at their site for a variety or reasons which management almost always neglect to consider. Despite their almost universal dislike by the staff of the firm, the managers tend to bring in Consultants & Contractors with more commonality then ever before. The main reasons that staff don't like consultants are upon examination something like common sense & some typical examples follow:

1. Consultants are seen by the full time staff as having no long term stake in the outcomes & their recommendations other than to extract as much money as possible from the firm
2. Consultants are seen by the full time staff as being paid a lot
3. They're seen to be given the most interesting, out of the routine work
4. They're seen to be telling the management of the firm what they want to hear or they tell the management of the firm what is just totally obvious to those at the operational level, but the management of the firm don't want to hear this type of information from the operational staff.

Full time staff are very often skeptical of the work, results & findings of consultants who are very often seen to be "Taking the Boss' Watch to Tell Then the Time", quote that you'll very often hear with regard to the use of Consultants, especially Management Consultants. Consultants are also seen as charging a lot of money & being paid high rates by the firm to tell the management of the firm information that was obvious to the staff at the operational level anyway & because the management of the firm are completely out of touch with the operational level, they had to be told it by somebody outside the firm & it's at this point that I'm reminded of the "Cow from Out of Town" story that I mentioned earlier. The

168

"Cow from Out of Town" syndrome is usually a very strong factor in the use of Consultants by the management of the large company.

Another factor with the use of consultants in large firms is that it's seen by the staff of the firm as being a chance for the consultants to get their foot in the door of the firm. For the staff of the firm it means that the most interesting work that would be out of the ordinary or the work that would allow them to grow the most in their careers is to be taken by somebody else & for the firm, the consulting form may be charging very high fees for something that their own staff could be doing unless the consulting firm is held under control. This effect can be particularly strong if the consultants are engaged on a "time & material" basis, because there's a definite incentive for the consultants to find work to increase their revenue & some consultants are very expert at finding work since it's been instrumental in their career advancement for many years. Many consultants also have little awareness of the long term implications of their work & recommendations, since many of them are thinking about their next assignment & they're not focused on the longer term, especially because they are typically measured quarterly on their utilization, so there is great incentive for the consultant to maximize the short term revenue that can be extracted from the customer with the detriment being felt in the longer term & many o the staff of the firm are aware of this point. I've heard it said many times words to the effect of: "I don't like consultants because they don't have to live with their own recommendations" & this is a very true criticism of many consultants.

The one exception to these points & arguments is the "hard edged" technical consultant because these types of consultants are typically brought in for a set period of time or to undertake some specialised piece of work. I have worked myself in this type of capacity & have generally found myself very well received by the staff of the firm, in fact because you're a technical expert you actually earn some measure of respect before you've even started work because people think of technical work in real terms, it's something that they can easily understand the scope, the problem & the solution, even if they lack the skills to get from the start to end themselves. In these circumstances you can find that you'll get a lot of help & cooperation from the staff of the firm, because if you're working in this type of capacity you're being seen as being productive & helpful not only to the management of the firm but also making every day work easier for the staff of the firm too.

The different type of consultants evoke very different reactions from the staff of the firm, before embarking on being a consultant yourself you have to think about this aspect because this will affect every single day of your working life. You can never expect that the staff of the firm that you're working with will like you & be happy to work together with you because you're a consultant, in fact quite the reverse will be true.

Scope

One thing that evokes major response from any consultant that's experienced & spent their time "earning their stripes" is scope. What are they there for & more importantly, what are the deliverables that are expected from them at the end of their assignment with the customer. These two issues may on the surface sound so terribly simple that it almost seems to be ridiculous that they even be mentioned but I've seen nothing cause more trouble for the consultant themselves & their management & also the customer than these issues.

I remember back to a time that I was sent to the Philippines to work for a large & very reputable company on a short term assignment & as is often the case the trip was organized by the office in Singapore which means that the customer was several hours flight from the management of my firm who had organised the whole deal. In fact it was also several weeks since the management of my firm had been to the site & so the knowledge of what was going on was several weeks old at a time when a lot of progress & change was ongoing. I'd just "rolled off" from a project & had very little time to prep[are but then again there wasn't much scope to prepare either since there's had been very little information forthcoming as to what was to be done for the client other than "you're to see what effort it would take for them to perform an upgrade to the next version of the software, be warned they're using a hardware platform that is known to be troublesome for us with our software" & so I met the other consultant who was to work with me on this job in Singapore in transit & then we went to the Philippines. I spoke to my colleague on the way from Singapore to the Philippines about what it was we were actually going to be doing & to my astonishment she has as little idea as I did & so with that I prepared to make this trip up as we went along.

The first day we arrived at the client site to begin to determine the upgrade effort only to find the customer mid way through the actual upgrade themselves !& it was immediately obvious that the entire trip was going to be redundant if we didn't change scope as soon as possible. I contacted the manager of the Singapore office who had organsied the whole thing & I asked him what it was exactly that he'd sold to the customer thinking he'd tell me & then we would probably sort out something from there, but the response was "what do you usually do in these situations? What would you normally deliver? & what would you normally do?" & it became obvious to me that the management had in fact no idea what it was they'd sold the customer & what it was that we were to deliver. This may sound like very unique circumstances but you'd be surprised how often you find yourself in this situation & I would expect that most consultants would come across this at least once per year that they're working due mainly to sales staff that sell things that they're not really understanding themselves to customer who aren't so sure what they need & they're relying upon the professionalism of the sale staff involves to make recommendations to help their business. In Asia where the sales/customer relationship tends to be ongoing & long lasting this relationship works well but when the USA model of making numbers in two quarters or you're out is introduced there is incentive for the sales staff to conduct themselves in a manner which would not normally be acceptable in Asia but which may be acceptable in the USA. Again we see the clash of cultures firmly happening.

Once I realised that I had to fix the situation or nobody else would my colleague & I set about attempting to define a scope that would be acceptable to both of us, our management & also remain a useful deliverable to the customer & from that point onwards the trip was without incident, but on this occasion we were saved by a customer that was not only reasonable but also very fair & able to use our services in a different way from which was were originally envisaged to work with them. Had this not been the case then the whole trip would have been a disaster. So some key recommendations come from this story. Not only is it important to have in advance what your scope of work with the customer is going to be, but also you need to know & understand what the deliverables are to be also. Once you're on site the very first thing you do after the usual pleasant introductions is to confirm with the customer their understanding of what the scope of work is to be done & what the deliverables are to be, not just the content but also the format, such as proformas to be used if any, written or presentation or both & also the theme & intended audience of the deliverables to give you some guide as to how it is to be written. This way you can maximize the chance that you outputs will be accepted by the customer, but not also that they will be accepted but that they will provide real value for money to the customer since often the same content reported in different ways can mean the difference between success & failure from the customer's viewpoint.

The other major issue with the subject of scope is the issue of "scope creep", that is, the customer ask for more & more & the amount of work tends to grow as time goes along. For the consultant & also the consulting company this issue is the number one dilemma in every day life because once a deal is made & the contract is signed the customer almost invariably will then set about trying to beak the contract but the use of scope creep. It's often very innocuous, such as; "While you're working on this program, can you add this, this & this, it shouldn't take very long" & often it doesn't take very long, but once you get hundreds of add-ons which can often happen during a project then problems can be made from the point of view of making project deadlines & also from the point of view of losing money for the form undertaking the implementation. This aspect of scope & running projects is often the bane of Project manager's lives since they're eternally grappling with the issue "how much work should I do for free to keep the customer happy, since every time I accept more work I risk the deadlines & the budget of the project". Of course this issue is like "how long is a piece of string", there's no always right & always wrong answer, but one thing is always right, saying "No" to the customer will lead you down the path of the customer feeling you're not trying to help them achieve their business needs & eventually you'll be removed off site often as soon as your contract has completed its term & then saying "Yes" to the customer will almost certainly com promise deadlines & budgets.

Projects

For the Consultant there are many types of projects & many type of assignments than you can end up being put onto & while they're always "sold" to as being beneficial to your long term career, the truth of the matter may be that this is always not the case. You should always be suspicious when you're approached to do something that is a "unique career growth opportunity" because these are the golden words than are used to cover up something which you really might not want to get involved with.

In the IT world, any project that has to do with the upgrade of legacy system is probably a ticket to nowhere. In the IT industry you're paid & promoted on your knowledge off new technology & so matter what the circumstances you really don't want to become involved with anything that has to do with legacy systems & especially the maintenance of legacy systems. There are very clear financial reasons for this also, because legacy systems are thought of by the management of the firm as something old that's had it's money spent on it & so costs have to be minimized on legacy systems because they're usually not core to the business. As a result staff who are linked with legacy systems have to have their costs as low as possible also & that include wages & so while you might be doing the firm a big favour undertaking such a job, there's every likely hood that this favour will not be repaid by the firm in the longer term because your knowledge of new technology will suffer

& you'll be though of as linked to the old systems that have to have their running costs minimized.

Firms are much more eager to spend money on new system & projects that will install new software because there's usually some kind of cost benefit that's been done to justify the purchase of the software in the first case & the firm accepts that they have to pay some large sums of money to get new systems working. Under these circumstances you can do well by undertaking the project because you'll learn new skills & you'll be participating in a project that will yield big financial returns to the firm. If they firm doesn't replay you financially afterwards then at least you'll have some good new skills to take somewhere that will pay for them & there's always the chance that you'll have to do this anyway after the project because there might not be a traditional line position for you after the project winds up anyway because many firms don't really plan for this.

Your individual role on the project will also great effect on the benefit that you can derive from a project. Of course you can't expect to start as a Project manager but you should be looking for some type of reasonable growth on your career as the time goes along. There is risk that if you stay with the same firms that you'll be given the title "Expert" which can in some ways hamper your career development, because once considered an expert then you'll be given the same types of work on subsequent projects. This can be a blessing in hard times because you'll be considered a valuable asset to the firm that should be retained but in the boom times this can be a problem as it can be difficult to break out from the expectations that everyone has of you & your position & it is essential that you do break out from this in order to go up the ladder to the Team Leader positions & then the Project Manger positions that will come in time. Being an expert for too long can mean that you're not learning the diverse skills sets that are required for the more senior positions.

One over riding thing to remember is that if you're working in a line position & you're offered the chance to work on a special project for a length of time of more than several months, then there's a good chance you'll have position at the end of it & that you may even be forced into redundancy. If you're going to learn very valuable new skills that you leverage from into other roles in other firms then this may well be worth thinking about but if this is not the case then there will be no purpose to accepting the role & there are a great many projects that happen in many firms that are not worth accepting, they help the company, but they won't help you in the longer term.

Customer Organised Travel

As a consultant there's one thing that's almost guaranteed; you're going to spend a lot of time away from home, from your family, boyfriends, girlfriends & husbands & wives & as such travel policies of the firms that you work for will be increasingly more important to you as time goes on in your career because coming back to a nice hotel after work is one of the small privileges that you'll have when you're away from home. Most firms have some type of travel policy detailing which hotel you're to stay in, which airlines to fly with, which class you'll fly on the airlines, maybe you'll fly Business Class if the flight is over a time limit such as eight or 10 hours? Some firms use per diems to reduce the paper work, so use reimbursement of actual expenses, the rules vary from firm to firm, but in my experience most firms have very sensible, realistic & very fair policies written & distributed to their staff. One thing that is often not mentioned in these travel policies is the fact that the sales staff, when they're negotiating their deals with the customer are only too willing to negotiate away your employment conditions if it means they can make more money elsewhere & gather a commission & that means that although there will often be written travel policies expect that there will be times when you'll be asked to deviate from them.

The one single most suspicious thing to watch out for is when you're told to go to a site & when you ask where to stay or when to make your booking you're told that ominous one liner; "Customer

Organised Travel" !!! even now after 11 years of consulting this send shivers down my spine as I recollect what has actually happened the times I've been told this, but at the same time it's some times not as bad as it sounds & can often be quite alright (but in my experience this is less than 20% of the time). What "Customer Organised Travel usually means is:

- Discounted plane tickets that can't be changed or cancelled booked for you to fly as off peak times ensuring long layovers & early or late take offs.
- Accommodation at "B" grade hotels or even motels that won't have 24 hour room services, digital PABX phone systems so you can't dial in & they won't be member of any Frequent Flyer schemes.
- On some occasions it means that the customer will rent a house for several of you which means that not only do you have to "put up with your colleagues" at work but you also have the "pleasure" of their company after work also. This is particularly unpleasant if some of you have very differing home life habits which is often the case with Consultants. I know, Consultants have some very strange personal life habits.

This reminds me of the time when I had such a situation in New Zealand where I was working in a new job & as such I didn't have the "clout" to argue against the "Customer Organised Travel" & the other consultants of the firm had the good sense to avoid the project in question & so myself & another colleague were pushed into this situation. The project Manager who was also from our firm but from the New Zealand office had his own very set ways of doing things such as he was obsessed by home cooking, he absolutely hated to eat out, even at lunch time & would cut his own lunch & he also hated to watch TV in the evening. Mind you, I don't mind each having their own personal habits when they're traveling for work & I'll be the first to admit that I have mince, such as I'm the type of person that orders pizza at 2:30am in a hotel & plays heavy music at all hours, which my house mates no doubt enjoyed as much as I did. But this manager went beyond having his own little habits but rather attempted to impose them onto the others on the project. It was like being in First Grade at school, where you're told what you have to do all the time & the customer & the Project Manager were able to exert substantial controlling pressure on everyone involved which resulted in substantial resentment, dissatisfaction & the situation now where several consultants will simply refuse to ever work for the Project Manager in question ever again & one resignation from the firm in question was also experienced.

All of this pain & heartache was involved because the firm allows their own travel policies to be bent to the point where working on the job was not pleasant for those involved. Simple adherence to the policies & the norms of the firm would have avoided all of these issues & cases such as this are often seen in the consulting world.

On the other side of the coin I have had experience of customer organised travel where the outcome has been very good & I worked once for an Electricity Company that insisted on their own bookings to save money & while I did stay in hotels that weren't major chains or brand names they were nevertheless very nice & so there was no adverse issues at all in these cases, but cases like this are indeed the minority. "Customer Organised Travel" usually means that the sales staff have cut a deal which means that you're going to be asked to stay in conditions that would usually be totally unacceptable to the firm's travel policies & usually totally unacceptable to yourself, I myself am immediately very suspicious when I hear the phrase as any consultant should be.

Project Results – Always "Success"

Results of the work of Consultants is often a very difficult thing to define & measure & what is "good" to one person may not be so "good" to another, it's all a matter of perspective.

One thing that the major consulting firms keep in mind is that they must always deliver on time because for most customers the running of projects especially for IT is something that is not their core business & the cost per day of the average IT project is very high & so, for the customer there is nothing worse than things running over their delivery date because this translates directly into money that lots of firms are very wary of, especially in difficult times. The running over of delivery dates is one sure way to ensure that your firm will not be engaged again by a customer so many firms will do everything they can to deliver on time, even if the actual deliverables are completely worthless, they'll always deliver on time, but the really worrying part of this equation is that the deliverables are often so rushed in order to make the delivery schedules that they are in fact worthless. Once this has happened then the "witch hunt" happens as to the worth of the work done, the value that it has achieved for the firm & the competence of the staff that had undertake the work in the first place.

No doubt after such an exercise the consulting firm in question immediately start sprucing that the whole exercise has been a wonderful success for everyone involved & the newspapers are called to witness & report on the huge & incredible "success" that has occurred while the poor customer I left to wonder what it is they actually have & wonder whether it is in fact a worthwhile result & what value it is to them. Some customers are left wondering if there's something wrong with them because they don't really understand what it is they've been left with, but there's no question that the completion of a project is a cause for celebration amongst the various participants that were undertaking the work involved, to do anything less would be an admission of guilt. So it's far to say that in the land of the Consulting Firm, every project is always successful, no matter how totally useless the final results.

OK Finished, Let's Go

Another issue when it comes to Consulting Firms is the lack on continuity that comes with major projects. Consulting Firms are usually engaged for a set period of time or for asset series of deliverables & whether the deal is fixed price or time & materials, the end game is the same… The Consulting firm will fulfill it's contractual obligation, get paid & leave at some point in time, after of course trying to stay for as long as possible, trying to generate as much billable work as possible whilst working for the client. Once the Consulting Firm has gone, what happens next? Often, the answer to this question is "nothing" unfortunately.

Many firms these days are running so lean that they have in fact lost the capability to do anything new at all. People are loaded up with so much work, that when there's a new project they simply can't take on additional work load, nor can they leave their old work behind because it still has to be done & many employees will actively resist working on projects of fixed duration because there's always the issue of what happens to somebody if they leave their current job for say 12 months to work on something else & then somebody else is trained in their original work in order to provide the "backfill" necessary? Unfortunately the original employee has nothing really left for them at the end of the project & the new staff member has all the recent knowledge for the original position & so the firm will not want to remove the "backfill" that had originally happened. Often the staff member is pushed & pulled from one place to another as the firm attempts to find something for them to do & eventually the staff member leaves of the firm will retrench them as not being required anymore.

Another thing to consider when the Consulting Firm leaves is that they often don't have people to train working with them, often despite their requests because there simply isn't anybody. The customer is running so lean that they have nobody to spare & the customer staff don't want to be removed from their much more secure line positions anyway into something project oriented & so when the Consulting Firm leaves & their staff are scattered to the next projects then there's often a knowledge vacuum left behind & nobody knows what to do, what happened or what to do to fix the situation.

This lack of continuity is a factor in almost every major Project that I have ever seen undertaken. Some Consulting Firms could be accused of doing this intentionally in an attempt to maximize their revenue from the customer, while other do it unintentionally &

some actively attempt to avoid this situation by requesting customer to staff to work with them, but the problem arises anyway because the customer can't spare the staff &/or the staff are unwilling to work on project type work anyway. But the real issue is that Consultants can recommend anything they like, but they nearly always don't have to live with the consequences of their actions.

The Bench

For Consultants themselves, nothing is more daunting than "The Bench" in that it can spell unemployment at an instant. It really means that you've finished one consulting assignment, you're now waiting for the next & you're not really scheduled to do anything specific.

There are many Consulting Firms that run along the lines of six weeks on the bench & you're looking for another job & this is driven by the fact that many firms in the USA have to give quarterly reporting to their respective stock exchange & some of the main figures that the Financial Analysts look at to give indication as the "Real Value" of shares (whatever that is anyway) are a lot of financial rations "per head", such as "Revenue per Head", "Fixed Costs per Head", so many firms madly cull their staff nearing the end of the reporting period in order to make these "per Head" figures look as palatable as possible for the financial analysts & those on "the Bench" are most likely to be victims to this as many customer like to have the same staff working on their project, so those on long term assignments are generally given a degree of safety.

"The Bench" also becomes more of an issue as the economy slows down because as people finish work there's little for them to go to & so the number of those on the bench will typically grow & it's those that have been there the longest that are most at risk. The way to most easily avoid this is to get yourself onto a long term engagement when the economic cycle looks bad & this can typically be done by lowering your rates at the right time in return for a long term engagement. Remember that economic cycles can go for years, so you would have to get commitments such as two years or so for this strategy to work properly. Unfortunately many Consultants don't the free reign over the hourly rates charged to customers & so they're at the mercy of the economy & the bench itself & being unable to attempt to drive up demand with lower rates they're at the mercy of generally inflexible company policies that will mean week on "The Bench" & then eventual redundancy in poor times. A good short term strategy is to use your accumulated Annual Leave if you have any, but not right away, stay on the bench for a few weeks before doing this as many firms to do report those one leave as being on the "Bench Report" back to Management because Annual Leave is an entitlement that is considered to be normal business & also many firms start to pay very close attention to those who have been on "The Bench" for more than six weeks or so, so every four weeks, take a week's leave, just to try & remove yourself from too much attention at a time when you don't want attention This might not save your job, but it will buy you time to find another job when times are tough.

Government Providing an Invisible Trading Environment to "Help" Business

Government Policy

Should the Government be invisible to Business & the Public? Or should they intervene as required to prevent market distortions from occurring? Or should they play a highly active part on the management & running of the economy at both the Micro & Macro level? Anybody who can answer this question has just solved all the world's economic problems.

The "Small Government" model which is that preferred in the USA is one where most of the vital services are contracted out & that there's a strong "User Pays' train of thought through the process. Also, the general population does not really went the Government to interfere with the daily lives & would see the strong intervention of the Government as an unnecessary invasion or privacy. This approach & this desire from the general populace actually helps the Government decision makers in that they're not required to attempt to pick the "winners" & the "losers", those who will benefit & those who will miss out or those who will be taxed more heavily then their share I order to pay for Government policy. This type of expectation from the general population is one of the main reasons why the USA has been so very successful in the area of Globalisation, because the population is more or less happy to let the free markets determine things & to let the Government only intervene when there is apparent market distortions or when one small group is being hit unduly hard by the market forces.

Japan is at the other end of the spectrum where the general populace is sued & expects the Government to intervene at all kind of levels on all kinds of issues. When the population has this level of expectation then there a re a lot of demands on the Government & there's also a lot of demands on the economy of that country also. The Government policy maker are forced to pick "winner" & "losers" because there's can never be enough money in the economy to make everyone a "winner". Once their winner/loser process is undertake then there's the issue of how much to support the "winners' & how much to penalize the "losers" this is very critical to difficult for many Governments because there is the risk that the "losers' will go elsewhere & the Government policy maker has to understand this very well when determining the level of "punishment" the "loser" will receive.

If economies were truly isolated from each other then the Governments of the respective countries would be free to do what they like with regard to economic policy, but the fact that people can move from one country to another, business can move from one country to another, profits can shift from one country to another & the fact that Globalisation of the world' economies is marching on relentlessly, means that there is an increasing amount of "Accountability" that Governments must face in the marketplace as a result of their decisions. They are simply not free to act anymore, because in many situations the action of one Government in one area will force the reaction of another, possible in the same area or possible elsewhere in a seemingly unrelated area as an act of retaliation. Decisions are now made keeping in mind that the world is now a kind of Oligopoly in many major areas. Major areas of importance typically have a few major players that work as oligopolies, while issues of lesser importance typically have a larger number of smaller players & more closely resemble the free market.

Free Trade

Free Trade has meant that for many, the ability to acquire cheaper products from overseas has come true as this was the main argument for the opening of trade back in the 1960's in many Western Countries. At this time many countries "hid" behind very high tariffs to stop other counties from taking their markets & their jobs, but at the same time this policy ensured that there would be inefficient allocation of resources amongst the nations. Countries which had natural advantages in certain industries could do nothing to exploit the situation & they could do nothing to efficiently use resources & prevent other countries from inefficiently using resources to achieve the same ends.

Increase in Living Standards was the catch cry at the time when this policy of dropping tariffs was introduced & in the very short term it was true, but not many countries at the time said "Your living standards will increase because products will be cheaper, but at the same time you might lose your job if you're working in an industry that's not really internationally competitive" & it was certainly the case that the large majority of workers in most Western countries didn't realise this would be the side effect & it's probably also the case that many politicians didn't think the long term consequences through either, because politicians often don't think too far beyond the next election & at the time, the dropping of tariffs & the introduction of cheaper imports from other countries to raise the living standard would have been an election winner.

Free Trade & "Globalisation" have to a large extent become synonymous to a large extent these days as countries clamour over each other to establish "Free Trade" agreements & as Europe forms one big giant Free Trade agreement in response to the major geopolitical advantage that the USA has held for the past 200 years. The USA has always been in the envious position of controlling effectively the majority if a continent with vast resources & enemies that were much less powerful than itself, allowing it to prosper economically while Europe spent the past 200 years fighting amongst themselves resulting in slower economic progress as a whole compared with the USA. With the only really serious attempts to unify Europe being Napoleon & Hitler's drives for domination, but since these drive meant the subjugation of a number of peoples then the resistance to these attempts were so strong as to break them before they had even started. This time however Europe has realised its position & the damage that continual in fighting has caused to their economic development over the past centuries, with the exception of some of the newly emerging nations such as the former Yugoslavia where the vehement nationalism of the past still prevails to an extent. Despite this final realised of the benefits of the union, the USA still holds advantage geopolitically in being more or less a unified people speaking a single language (although this could be questioned now due to the preponderance of Spanish in the southern parts of the country). This allows workers to move in accordance with demand

& supply of labour in a much more seamless manner, for example, plant layoffs on the East Coast may see some workers move to the West Coast if conditions we re better there & this is quite simple for the worker, it's the same country & same language, same educational standards etc, but the work in Europe moving fro the East of the Union to the West or vice versa represents language difference s& so there are still natural obstacles to deal with although these may well be reduced from those of the past & these difficulties will form a type of economic entry barrier to the taking up for example of tax incentives to promote growth in various areas & other initiatives that may come to pass as time goes on. Perhaps the Esperanto concept wasn't such as bad idea of a common language to bind the world together & it may be that the creation of Esperanto was a concept before its natural time.

Taxation Policy

Taxation policy can have a huge effect on the work of individuals in differing industries as does the factor of whether the Government power prefers a Macro or Micro approach & how favourable the Government is to the idea of Globalisation. Some would argue that it's the philosophy differences of the politics of the parties in power that can make differences to the individuals affected by the decision, but I would argue that Globalisation is bigger than politics of the individual nation now & whether the government be to the left or to the right, it really makes little difference to the lot of the average work in the long term, although short term differences may well be apparent.

Many Slight-Right wing Governments prefer the combination of mostly Macro Management along with a Lower Tax Regime. This has its merits in that this model fits the Globalisation model well, where countries compete more on the Macro level & companies have to work within the Macro framework set by their respective governments.

I this type of environment those occupations that have global markets can thrive such as the IT sector because there is little regulation on this industry around the world & it's no surprise that this industry is one of the most competitive & global in it's viewpoint. The loser in this type of environment is the worker who competes against the low cost worker in other countries & this is typically those with a lower skill base or an older industry with older skill sets such as the textile worker. Governments often attempt to assist this type of work with subsidies to their industries in the form of direct cash subsidies or tax incentives as these are consider much more "pure" to the open Governments today than tariffs, but tariffs still exist to achieve these ends. What many Governments struggle with today is this situation & the effect that it has on the revenue base because as Governments take money to support those workers suffering the effects of this type of situation they in effect take the money from those doing better under these conditions. The "Robin Hood" theory of "Take from the Rich to Give to the Poor" all seems to be very noble & there is no doubt that the motive is noble the long term result is that those being equalised down for the common good of society start to look elsewhere, perhaps for a place where there are no textile works that have to be subsidised & as a result lesser taxes to pay. This "looking around" can also be clandestine in it's nature not being so much a physical shifting of the work effort, but much more often a more subtle effect being the transfer of profits due to the effect of "Transfer Pricing" which many firms actively engage in today.

Transfer pricing is where the profit is in effect shifted to another country where the tax regime has lower rates. This is very easily done in an operation which has offices into two companies. Imagine for instance that we have office in Australia with a company tax rate of about 30% & another in Singapore with a company tax rate of about 10%. If you're running your business to maximize your profits you'll don some thing like:

Manufacture the item in Australia - Cost = say $10

Sell Item to Singapore Office at Cost price of $10

Sell Retail in Singapore at Sales Price of $20

Profit = $10 in Singapore so only $1 in tax paid in Singapore, no tax paid in Australia

Also, it doesn't make any difference if the item is made in Singapore & imported into Australia:

Manufacture the item in Singapore - Cost = say $10

Sell Item to Australia Office at Sale price of $20

Sell Retail in Australia at Sales Price of $20

Profit = $10 in Singapore so only $1 in tax paid in Singapore, no tax paid in Australia

In any event Australia misses out completely from the revenue generated & the low tax Singapore picks up the revenue for their Government to spend. Many high tax countries are either oblivious to this situation or for left wing political reasons they choose to ignore it, but the reality is that for high tax countries a lot of revenue is lost this way.

Slight Left-Wing Government tend to prefer to manage the economy using a combination of Micro Economics & tax policy. They like to try & pick "winner" & "losers" in the quest for Government funding & the poor textile worker is usually a high priority for this type of Government which is typically elected on the platform of supporting those who are not as well off as those who have managed to benefit from Globalisation.

The problem is that again all the same issues are encountered, those being equalized down for the common good of society start to look around for regimes to go to where they're not equalized to the same extent. The differing focus of the left & right win Governments makes little different to the outcome, the difference is more in the nature of the assistance to the recipient than to the payer of the tax.

One of the key differences for the left wing Government is that they have tendency to pick Industry based winners & losers with some industries being equalized down for the common good & so again the same effects are seen to apply in that those being equalized down for the common goods looking around for lower tax regimes, but this time in a more industry based way than under the right wing Government, where the approach causes a more individualistic approach to the situation. Nevertheless the loss of the taxation revenue base is the final outcome in those economies where the free market is interfered with too much. Many Western Governments shave this very issue high on their agendas because their revenue bases are slowly being deteriorated by the flight of talented individuals & promising & profitable industries to other places where they are not used as "Cash Cows" for the Government to extract revenue from.

Centre of the road political parties suffer from exactly the same symptoms & so we're left with only those on the outer right & outer left being able to give themselves direction in this matter, but the Governments of this type are really very unlikely to embrace Globalisation with any gusto & as a result they would tend to be left behind by technology as the greater work union operation under the auspices of Globalisation will have infinitely more resources available to them over time to advance while the closed isolated economy could never hope to advance at the same rate. Good examples of this is how the USSR attempted to isolate itself from the world except for it's various allied & targeted areas of military interest. Over time they fell behind & the rate of falling behind, be it technologically & economically began to accelerate to the point where the Government itself realised something had to be done. The same applies to other smaller countries like Iraq, which required some outside "assistance" in removing the introverted Government that was in power there.

Monopolies

Government Monopolies used to be everywhere in the Western world, power, water, gas, phones, airlines were all typically either Government run or they were licensed by the Government & the Government maintained a very high level of interest in the running of these types of organizations, but one thing in the past was true most of the time. Most of these organizations were very inefficient in their use of resources because they were run by the Government & there were so many political agendas that the organizations weren't free to pursuer their publicly stated objectives without massive interference from their Governments.

The demise of the Government run monopoly is largely a result of the Taxation policy argument sin the preceding Chapter. Governments simply don't have & won't have the money to subsidise these types of operations anymore & this will have a really huge impact on the workers & staff in these industries. Typically jobs in these industries were thought of as not that exciting but very safe, secure & steady employment, that could always be relied upon & so these industries were the haven for those who were perhaps a little more risk adverse than the community as a whole & this represented a large portion of the population that were ready to sacrifice possible higher wages in the private sector in return for the security of employment these organizations represented. These days this is not true at all & so now there are entire industries of people that have this risk element hanging over their heads to a level that they're not comfortable with. I have done a lot of work in the Utilities Industries consulting for Software Companies & from what I've seen the past years is the furthest thing that you could ever imagine from stable employment. Government Sales, Mergers, Splits ups, every kind of conceivable management structure & methods of management have been employed & this has been the case in some industries for more than 10 years to the point where these organizations are just not stable employment of any kind anymore & yet their salaries have typically not kept up with those in the Private Sector when it comes to salary growth. If you were working in these industries now you would really have to be wondering whey you're staying there as I've seen massive staff cuts & massive staff turnover. In fact, this in itself opens opportunities because these firms still typically hang onto their old outdates Human Resources policies which haven't kept up with the changing times & so promotion from within is sometimes a high priority for these firms & with massive staff turnover there is opportunity for quicker than would have been the case career progression "up the ladder" as people leave & take early retirement in the industries.

In the future we can only see the process of Government selling off their major assets continuing & in many cases to reduce opposition to this, many Government shave introduced competition in advance of the sell off of the Government Assets in order to "wake up dissident groups such as Unions" that things will change no matter what. In fact, in many cases the opening of an industry to competition removes Union power to a large extent because it quickly becomes apparent to all concerned that things must change from how they were in the past otherwise the original firm that was the old Government monopoly will cease to exist & then there won't be any jobs at the old firm at all for anyone. At this point workers are usually only too happy to make changes in order to save their jobs & the Unions are willing to cooperate with the Management of the firm in order to save as many jobs as possible, when it may be better for the individual worker to leave & go the new entrants in the market, since these new entrants are typically less Unionised & those in positions of demand would typically be able to secure employment on better wage deals than they could have under the old system, but many of the lower skilled workers will be attempting to hold onto the old practices, but the holding of old practices will mean the demise of the firm in the long term.

The Economy Affects You, Your Job & Your Potential Growth

The NASDAQ Crash 2001-2002 / The USA Shudders & then Recovery Begins

Nothing has affected the I. T. industry as much as the NASDAQ crash of 2001 after the boom years of the 2000 bug which had caused firms to spend inordinate amounts of money to insure that they would not have problems on that magical first of January, 2000 the growth in I. T. industry in the use letting up to these had just been phenomenal at the time I felt myself that I was in the middle of the bubble something that was so big and out of control that there was nothing that I will could do or say that would affect anything but the same time line use of myself that we would pay for this one day and the day of reckoning was really September 2001 the IT industry had been in decline for most of 2001 although the decline had been fairly slow and steady, then September 911 happened and then the decline became a stampede people shut down any prospect of spending money on new projects and job openings to simply dried up as companies were reluctant to hire new staff in the current economic conditions of the time by myself soar a lot of colleagues who were retrenched during this time and who had at that point in time very little prospect of getting a new job because there was simply no jobs to be had the times of double digit growth of employment in the 1990's had definitely finished at least for the time being and possibly for always as the industry begins to mature. Remember not every industry can keep on growing at a fast pace forever there's a time of growth stabilization, maturity and then later on in the longer term decline as some other technology comes to take its place and there is nothing special or wonderful about the I. T. industry that would make it an exception to these rules. It could be argued that the slowdown of 2001 was something of a natural slowdown that may have happened anyway to the maturing of the IT industry but at the same time the activities of September 11 certainly acted as a catalyst to the slowdown process at that point in time.

2001 was probably the slowest the in the I. T. industry for a very long time as I mentioned earlier; colleagues that I had gone to work with had been retrenched we're experiencing extreme difficulty in getting new jobs, some taking as long as the whole year in order to find new positions while 2002 was only very slightly better and some market segments worse buttons others. There had been some recovery of some market segments although the recovery had been very patchy and one of the hardest hit areas was the CRM segment; an industry segment which had been the prize growth area during 1999 and 2000 and to many it'd become the next "golden cow" after that of ERP but when times became hard and money became scarce CRM became too much of a "nice thing to have" and so all the CRM vendors started to experience extreme drops in sales revenue and in response to this they started their cost cutting exercises which included the culling of large numbers of staff. Some of these staff were sapped up buying the ERP vendors who were still going business and some sort of consistent level although still quieter than the prior years but other IT staff was simply unable to get jobs and in my experience those with technical skills you could actually sit down and do hands on work and write code and convert data seem to get the jobs much easier than the business based consultants and the business analysts, the moral of this story is that if you have hard technical job skills then you have a measure of job stability in this environment. Because there were no new projects on offer, then the Project manager was the very hardest hit at this time. Only now 2003 did the industry begin to pick up although the pickup was initially patchy in some different market segments and the pickup has not exactly been a fast pickup, in fact quite the reverse the pickup has been quite slow but at least steady, but sitting now in 2007 the market has fully recovered an in fact suffering shortfall since many young people have now been "scared off" from pursuing a career in IT. Parents now tell their leaving school age children: "IT is no career; it's not stable".

Lemming Effect

We're So Different

One thing that customer tell you is that they're different. Every single customer that I've ever been to see say something like "We're so special & different because of this, this & this. See, nobody else is like this, so we need something very special" & nearly always this is totally untrue. Almost all customers in the same industry are almost exactly the same all the time & even between industries there is often very close similarities. You should always bear this in mind & the funniest thing to remember about this is that you've often been chosen to work with this customer because you had industry experience that they thought would be relevant to the work to be undertaken The challenge for you as a consultant is to treat the customer as if they are different, be response to their needs because this telling you that they're different is another way of saying "please give us you undivided attention", it's like a cry for help & your best efforts.

I'm reminded of the customer that told me they're so different when I went to meet them as a preliminary for a Sales Consulting role. I was to meet with the customer, talk with them about their business & the formulate some type of solution to present to them during the sales demonstration. We spoke to the major players in the firm, half of which told me that they're so different, the other half telling me that they're "pretty much the same" as the other firms in the industry?

The other thing to remember that that your experience in other firms is what the customer is paying for, if it was really true that they're so different then experience would count for nothing & this is almost never the case. This also is the case for packaged software, if it were the case that the firm was so totally different to the other of the industry then it would be pointless for them to buy packaged enterprise wide software such as an ERP or CRM system, but again this is almost never the case. Being different for the customer is more a state of mind & a way of telling the consultant to pay attention to detail, for the small things that might in fact be different. If the firm were in fact truly so totally different to the others in the industry they'd either be the clear market leader or they'd be on the way to bankruptcy & they would be looking to hire you as they'd be in a drastic cost cutting phase.

Industry "Best Practice"

Lots of firms in that is the best practice is something that they need to follow because everybody else is following industry best practices to but the issue arises as to what is industry best practice and it is on this point that many companies lose the way and fail to understand what he is that they actually trying to do

A lot of firms make the mistake of looking at the industry average and using this as the benchmark upon which to measure performance of both staff and also to up of the organisational as a whole but the idea of using industry average as a benchmark for performance and as a benchmark for which a per the business is actually quite flawed Because it is the business aiming for the industry average that will achieve the industry average and may in fact hamper any opportunity to perform above average

Other firms seek to achieve above average performance for the industry wide modeling themselves on the high achievers with in this industry in which they are operating but this also can be floored from time to time because the implementation of policies that are acceptable and successful in one firm may not mean that these same policies us successful in another firm this can need you to a number of factors but the main factors other cultural ones where policies that can be effectively implemented in one firm under one set of cultural conditions and can be successful under these cultural conditions may work extremely adversely under another set of different cultural conditions that would exist in other firms this is often overlooked by manages to attempt to implement trendy policies and procedures that other firms in the same industry are attempting to implement many manages themselves have their own

194

careers tied to the successful implementation of these trendy policies because once they have implemented these policies in one firm and they have this information on their resume then back quite capable of bringing this skill set elsewhere and say the issue becomes one of skilling the executive who has too much self interest in the proceeds rather than helping the firm as a whole and the people that are left to pick up the pieces of those loyal staff members who have stayed with the firm throughout the entire transition these other people who have to weigh in the long term effects and it is because of this type of approach that management has often taken in the past that many employees become cynical and especially distrustful of consultants that are brought in by the management to look at the operation of the firm

So best practice can drastically vary from one firm to another even within the same industry and even within, and operating parameters its it is extremely important that the management of the firm realise that this is the case and implement and plan accordingly but all too often in real life this is forgotten about as manages scramble in a frenzy to attempt to implement trendy plans trendy policies and trendy ideas that currently in the marketplace that other half buzz words that will help their ratio may look better and help them increase their earning power then next job with little or no fallen to the firm that they currently working full and little or no floor to the subordinate start for the working for them who will eventually end up having to wear the resolves for the foreseeable future

Final Thoughts

I hope this paperback is proved useful to the user perhaps not an everyday level but I do hope that it has been helpful to the reader on the more strategic longer term level on the kind of level where the reader is thinking what should I do my career where am I going what should I look for in order to help me get ahead one thing should I be avoiding wafting should I be looking towards one thing you should I be looking to turn to my advantage I hope that this paperback is in some way attempted to address all these issues and hopefully provide some insight and some useful answers to those who read this paperback

I do realise that there are some passages in this paperback that could easily be taken as the work of the skeptic and I guess that is partly true but at the same time I've tried to pay things in a totally down to earth and realistic manner without any of the glossy show business the company's a lot of the aspects that discussed in this paperback many firms attach a lot of glossy show business to a lot of what they do in order to try to make the firm look more attractive to prospective employees and also attractive to prospective customers and when this happens prospective employees and current employees are often forgotten in the rush to appeal to the market I do hope that a lot of employers read this paperback and bear in mind some of the message is contained within in order to provide to the staff something more resembling a good place to work by myself of working good places I've worked in bad places and I know what a difference it can make to your own life at home when you're working in a bad place and you can't see any quick and easy way to get out of that situation

For the employee I had this paperback has given you some ideas some things to think about and some ideas that will sit in the back of your mind and maybe jolted out to the forefront from time to time depending on what happens when you are and depending on what to see and do.

References / Bibliography

1. G. Orwell, "1984 Nineteen Eighty-Four", (Signet, New York, 1949).

2. I. Janis, "VICTIMS OF GROUPTHINK", (Boston: Houghton Mifflin, 1972).

Glossary

B2B	Business to Business
B2C	Business to Customer
CRM	Customer Relationship Management
ERP	Enterprise Resource Planning
Head Count	Number of Staff Working for the Firm
HR Department	Human Resources / Human Resources
IT	Information Technology
IS	Information Systems
MBA	Master of Business Administration
SI	System Integrator
SLA	Service Level Agreement